D0429129

Praise for
The Fixed Stars

"Wizenberg writes with a remarkable openness about being true to herself and to others. . . . This honest and moving memoir will enlighten and educate those seeking to understand their true selves."

—*PUBLISHERS WEEKLY* (STARRED REVIEW)

"*The Fixed Stars* is that rare thing, a groundbreaking, essential book about sexuality. Wizenberg's incisive, generous laying-bare of her own experience will make many readers feel seen, understood, and not alone. This book is a triumph."

—KATE CHRISTENSEN,
author of *Blue Plate Special* and *The Last Cruise*

"In *The Fixed Stars*, Molly Wizenberg tackles the ever-shifting issues of marriage, motherhood, and sexual orientation with the same compassion and unflinching honesty that have become the hallmarks of her writing. She makes the everyday extraordinary and brings depth and complexity to the bigger questions in life. A beautiful read."

—ERICA BAUERMEISTER,
author of *The Scent Keeper*

"An intimate account . . . beautifully written. . . . An essential addition that will resonate with fans of Wizenberg's earlier memoirs and anyone probing the complicated ways that sexuality and traditional family life overlap or diverge."

—*LIBRARY JOURNAL* (STARRED REVIEW)

The Fixed Stars

THE FIXED STARS

Molly Wizenberg

Abrams Press, New York

For credits, see page 244

Jacket © 2020 Abrams

Published in 2020 by Abrams Press, an imprint of ABRAMS.

Library of Congress Control Number: 2019939896

ISBN: 978-1-4197-4299-6
eISBN: 978-1-68335-892-3

Printed and bound in the United States

10 9 8 7 6 5 4 3 2 1

Abrams books are available at special discounts when
purchased in quantity for premiums and promotions as well
as fundraising or educational use. Special editions can
also be created to specification. For details, contact
specialsales@abramsbooks.com or the address below.

Abrams Press® is a registered trademark of
Harry N. Abrams, Inc.

ABRAMS The Art of Books
195 Broadway, New York, NY 10007
abramsbooks.com

Contents

Author's note

*This book is a memoir,
a work of nonfiction that relies
primarily on both my memory and
my interpretation of events.
In some cases, names and identifying
details have been changed to respect
and guard the privacy of others.*

I was grateful
for that, too,
the commonness
of my feeling, I
felt some stubborn
strangeness in
me ease, I felt
like part of the
human race.
———

—Garth Greenwell, "The Frog King"

Could

Have

1

The jury summons came in late spring. There's an optimism to bringing in the mail—a small, dinky optimism, but I like it. It's reliable. Leaning against the kitchen counter, I spread out my loot. Wedged between the electric bill and a glossy sheaf of coupons is the jury summons. It's a white trifold, stapled, with block letters announcing its contents. I split the staple from the paper with my thumb. There's a rhythmic thump behind me, probably June trying to liberate the bin of toys we keep wedged under the sideboard. The afternoons are stretching toward summer now, but the countertop is still cold under my elbows, the way cotton bedsheets are when you first climb in. The summons reads, TUESDAY, 8:30 A.M. We have a babysitter every Tuesday until five, and Brandon will be at the new restaurant site all day, supervising the buildout. If I've got to have jury duty, I guess a Tuesday's not bad.

The courthouse peers down a sloping grid of streets toward Puget Sound. I ride the elevator up and give my name to a woman in shoulder pads at the reception desk. There are already a few dozen people seated in the assembly room, recipients of the same summons. We wait. I don't mind; I've brought my laptop and a magazine. I don't want to wind up on a jury, but being stuck in this room presents the pleasant constraints of an airplane in mid-flight: there's nowhere to go and nothing else to do, so I might as well work.

The receptionist begins to read names, and mine comes halfway down the page-long list. I stand and join the crowd that's collecting in the entryway, where another woman appears, announcing herself as the bailiff. She hands us each a numbered sheet of paper in a plastic sleeve. We'll be going into the courtroom shortly, and we're to follow her to the seats in back. We follow her like ducklings, around a wall behind the judge's bench and into a fluorescent-lit courtroom. I'm pleased that it looks like all the ones on TV, though it's missing Sam Waterston. The judge has short feathered hair and wears black robes and a pair of drugstore reading glasses, over which she watches us enter. She gives off the aura of a successful real estate agent from the 1980s, a childhood friend's mom who served Lean Cuisine every weeknight without apology. There's a female prosecutor and two attorneys on the defense's side. The bailiff leads us past them, through a wooden gate, to our seats.

The attorneys stand one by one to introduce themselves and their clients. The prosecutor wears a tailored skirt suit, and the male defense attorney has a swoop of hair that lays across his forehead like a paper fan. The second defense attorney is a woman in a men's suit. I know it is a men's suit because of the way it hangs straight at her hips. When she rises to speak, a smile blooms shyly across her mouth. Her teeth are gardenia-white. She's said her name already, but I missed it.

The judge presents the case, and then the attorneys ask us questions in rotation, calling us by the numbers in our plastic sleeves, weeding us out. They explain that this process has a name, voir dire, and that they're looking to uncover our biases. There are so many of us, it takes hours. Finally, the prosecutor calls my number. She smiles and asks where I get my news. We banter a little about NPR. It turns out we're both Terry Gross fans. She asks what I do for a living, what kind of writer I am. I am a writer who listens to public radio. Of course I'll be eliminated.

But they're coming to the end of the numbers, and I'm still in the pew. They excuse another number, another. At the end of the day, there are eight of us left, and I'm given a new number, Juror #1, assigned to the first seat in the back row of the jury box. We're to reconvene the next morning.

*

I catch an early bus and find I have a half hour to spare. I've worn a linen dress that I bought a couple of years before June was born. Usually I only ever wear jeans, but now that I'm on a jury, I decide to look like someone who takes this seriously. I sit down in a stripe of weak sunlight on a bench outside the courthouse and pull out a thermos of coffee and my magazine from yesterday. The defendant is arriving, and he sits with his attorneys on a low wall outside the front door. I watch them over my magazine. They huddle like football players, eyes closed. It looks like they're praying.

The testimony takes four days. It's a civil disobedience case, and the judge has told us not to talk about it with anyone outside the courtroom, not even our families. We're not supposed to look up news stories about it or Google anyone involved. Each morning we wait in the assembly room, and the bailiff takes us to a restricted-access elevator at the back of the building, careful not to cross anyone else bound for the courtroom. I didn't want to be here, but since I am, I will do this right. I tune my body like an antenna, listen and take notes.

The woman in the men's suit has an accent, something approximately southern. I can't put my finger on it. I wonder how she wound up in Seattle. I wonder where in the city she lives. She's got a trustworthy haircut, what an insurance salesman might get in a midwestern barbershop. It's a lesbian haircut, I think. Her suit is the gray of spent charcoal, and the fabric swings loose around her legs when she walks. From my seat I can see her profile, the nose a little too large for its face, a pair of broken-in black cowboy boots under the table. I watch her wrists. They're slim, elegant, the bones delicate as songbirds. I could loop my fingers around her wrist and make the tips touch.

On the day that her client gives testimony, she stands up to question him and walks toward the jury box, stops a few feet from me. She rests her yellow lined pad on the half-wall that separates the jury from the courtroom, folds her hands, and rests them on top. Her wrists. I watch how the tendons move, taut as a cable-stayed bridge. Sweat prickles my palms. I'm relieved when she sits back down.

What is this? Am I attracted to her? I've never been with a woman, had only considered it once, and then only briefly. *Why am I looking at her?*

The next day she's not doing anything special, just sitting beside her client at the table, and I notice that I'm watching her again. This time she turns in her seat and looks at me. It's just for a second, and then we both look away, but not before something cold crackles up the back of my neck. I can hear my pulse in my ear.

She's caught me. She knows I was watching her.

Everyone must know it.

A second later: *Of course not. Don't be crazy.* It would be stupid to think she's noticed me at all. This is her job. To her, I'm a juror. Of course I would look at her.

But she's got to have noticed. I'm not looking; I'm watching. She's got to have noticed.

I know myself to be dense about certain things, moments and actions that other people tell me are obvious. I stare at people, forgetting that they might see me staring and think it's rude. It's not that I think they can't see me; it's that I do not think at all. I can never tell when a person is flirting with me, or when I'm flirting. Here's a liability for the owner of a restaurant: I cannot tell when someone is drunk. Unless it's formally declared and ratified by others present, like a UN resolution, I assume a person is just annoying or unusually friendly.

If I've noticed me watching, why wouldn't she?

What the fuck am I doing.

She's probably seen my wedding ring. If she has, she's read me. I see it now: a satin sash across my chest with the whole story embroidered on it. I'm straight, married for nearly a decade, with a house in the suburbs, a not-quite-three-year-old, a family dog, and two restaurants that I own with my husband. Shame creeps along my cheek like a spider.

When I cannot watch her, I think about watching her. I think all the time about it.

I leave the house each morning with my thermos of coffee, thinking. I walk down our street, turn the corner, walk a few more blocks, and board the bus, thinking. One morning mid-trial I catch the headline of a fellow bus rider's newspaper: the Supreme Court had ruled on *Obergefell vs. Hodges*, making same-sex marriage legal across the United States. I choke back a sob, elated, disbelieving. Then I want to cry for a different reason, and I cannot tell anyone why. I think about her wrists and her white teeth. I wonder what she thinks about me.

Then I remember not to think about that, because she probably doesn't think about me, and if she does, it cannot be good. I am a woman wearing a wedding ring while staring at a person who is not her spouse.

The judge is speaking again, and I'm not listening. I'm watching the woman in the suit. Under the crisp lapels of her jacket, there's a swelling across her chest, a softness that says *female*. I wonder what it would feel like to put my arm around her. Her shoulders would be solid, more substantial than my own. If I think on it, I can feel them under my triceps, sound as a fence. I wonder what she wears when she's not wearing this suit, on the weekends or after work. I wonder what her friends call her. I wonder what she would look like next to me in a photo.

I've had crushes since being with Brandon. A few, mostly little things, banal. We'd joke about them. For years, he nursed a crush on the actress Natalie Portman. It was like that. Safe. But I'd had another type of crush too, other men I'd wanted without saying a word. There were only one or two of them, but these men loomed over us. I never called his attention to their elephantine shadows. Telling him would have made them more real, made actual people out of these dark shapes, made distractions into danger. It would have frightened us both. Instead, I chipped away at the shadows privately, interrogated them into submission.

Do I want to be someone who cheats?

No. I don't want to be someone who would do that.

Am I willing to do that to Brandon?

No. He doesn't deserve that.

Can I get what I want by cheating, without also *getting what I* don't *want?*

No.

No, no. Always no.

Even if the conclusion had been a brief *yes*, which it never had, this fact would stop me: The lust would wear off. The sheen would dull. I knew it would. I'd still be me, just with a different set of problems.

Each afternoon when the judge dismisses us, I bolt from the building, fast-walk down the hill to the bus stop. My sandals slap the pavement on the downslope, left right left right, *who am I, who am I. Who* am *I?*

The vinyl bench seats of the bus are sticky with summer heat. I sit down, poke in my earbuds, think about what to make for dinner. I've missed June. We've had to get extra babysitting this week, a cost we hadn't budgeted for. I've hardly been around. Even in the evenings, I've hardly been around. Do I remember anything we've done, me and June? Me and June and Brandon? I've been thinking about the woman in the suit. That's what I remember.

I have to stop. I know the answers to the questions. They will end this.

Do I want to be someone who cheats?

No.

Am I willing to do that to Brandon?

No.

The sheen will wear off, and you know it.

Do I? I've never been with a woman.

Does that make a difference?

Maybe it does. What if it does?

You'd still be you, wouldn't you?

Would I?

The bus is too hot. The fabric under my arms is damp, and I can smell myself. Something is wrong with me.

But I don't have to tell anyone. Brandon doesn't have to know, remember? The woman in the men's suit doesn't either. She has no idea that a single glance in my direction, her eyes on my skin, would keep me awake all night, fantasizing.

It's my secret. I'll keep it here, with me. I can visit my secret whenever I want. Knowing this feels luxurious. That's the word for it. Luxurious. The place where I keep this secret is padded and dim, the feeling when you lie back in the bath and the water covers your ears. I can climb inside it anytime I want, anywhere—on the bus, in a swiveling chair in the jury box—and I can think of her. No one has to know.

The trial takes a week and ends on a Wednesday. The verdict comes down to minutia, and we are unanimous; the defendant is not guilty. I am certain that my vote to acquit has nothing to do with the fact that I've been watching the defense attorney in the men's suit. I know that my desire to assert this certainty has everything to do with the same fact. But I can go home now, put it behind me. Across the room, I watch the defendant light up with relief. I wonder if, at some point in the near future, I will feel relief like that.

For now, I have to memorize her. Now she will go home, back to her part of the city. I'd never seen her before a week ago, and I won't see her again. I wish this didn't make me feel desperate.

The formality of the courtroom has dissolved, and we're dismissed. We can walk wherever we want to walk in the courthouse, talk to anyone about anything. I text Brandon to let him know I'm done. He's working near home today, not near the courthouse, so I'll take the bus. *Let's meet for a quick drink*, he texts; he'll meet me along the bus route with his car. We've got the sitter until six. *Hurrah!* I type. *I can tell you about the trial.*

I walk out of the courtroom with the other jurors. We get to ride in the normal elevators now, and we're jumpy, unsure of how to be with one another. Outside the front doors, the air conditioning gives way to a blast of heat. My gut flips over when I see a huddle of people outside: the defense attorneys, their client, a few observers from the back of the courtroom. They applaud. The defendant reaches out, squeezes my shoulder. Behind him, the woman in the men's suit is standing in the half-shade of a small potted tree. She's taken off her jacket and rolled up the sleeves of her white shirt. It must have been starched at some point but is already drooping. I'm sweating in only a tank top. She steps toward me, and the sun explodes off the paving tiles. I raise my hand to shield my eyes.

Thanks so much, she says. We weren't sure how that was going to go, so this is a huge relief. She's smiling, and she offers her right hand, and we shake.

I'd looked at this hand so many times, but now that I touch it, the moment is over so fast that I can't feel anything. It occurs to me that with my left hand up at my brow, the diamonds along my wedding band must be winking in the sun like lighthouse beacons. I cross my arms, tucking my ring finger into the crook of an elbow.

I heard in voir dire that you're a writer, she says. Me too. I'm Nora, by the way.

Oh, wow, I squeeze out. Sweat is beading on my collarbone like a cheap necklace. What kind of writing do you do?

Mostly fiction, Nora says. She is a lawyer part-time; she took this case to help a friend. She pushes her hands into her pockets, rocks on her heels.

She's talking more than she has to. Is this flirting? Don't be an idiot. She couldn't see you that way. You're married. You're straight.

Nice, I say, and force a smile. My right eyelid twitches from squinting.

Cool, she says, like a normal person. She smiles back.

I've wanted this moment, thought about it for a week, but staying put takes effort. The sun is so bright that it stings, a warning heat. My eyelid is spasming wildly now.

It was nice to meet you, I manage. Maybe I'll see you around.

She nods, still smiling. Thanks again, she says. She's already pivoting on her heel, back to her client.

I turn fast, hoping she hasn't seen whatever my eyelid is doing, what my whole face must be doing. I aim myself at the bus stop and start moving, *who am I? who am I? who am I?*, all the way down the street.

When I get there, I've missed the bus, and the next won't come for fifteen minutes. I rest my tote bag between my ankles and lean my shoulder against the steel frame of the bus shelter, hoping to steady the twitch in my gut. There's a crowd of homeless men in front of the building across the street, their backs against its stone facade. I wonder if the stone feels cool in this heat. They must have been out here all day, while we sat in air conditioning. While I am forming this thought, Nora walks past them. She's slung her jacket over her shoulder, and a soft-sided briefcase hangs at her hip. She lowers herself onto an empty bench at the bus stop opposite mine. Her hair looks stringy with sweat, and there's a shadow under her eyes. She hasn't noticed me. I don't know what I'd do if she did. I look at the pavement.

My bus arrives. In case Nora has seen me, I make a show of my eagerness to leave, my detachment from the past week. I lock my eyes onto the bus door as it passes me, swivel my head extravagantly to follow it to the curb. I am a stage actor in a play about a bus stop. I step up through the folding doors and take the first open seat on the street side, where I can still see her. She's put in her earbuds now, leans forward, lets her hair hang. The bus lurches away from the sidewalk, and I watch her get smaller and smaller, until she disappears into the glare.

I could have yelled to Nora when I saw her. I could have caught her eye. Or she could have seen me, yelled to me across the street. There's a poem by Wisława Szymborska, "Could Have," about chance, fortune, and the flukes that often decide life and death. It begins, "It could have happened. / It had to happen. / It happened earlier. Later. / Nearer. Farther off. / It happened, but not to you."[1]

In another iteration, I could have lived it differently. In some other life, I could have stood next to her in a photo.

But what about Brandon? What about June? I swing like a pendulum from sadness to relief, sadness to relief. A disaster averted; it could have happened, but it didn't.

The bus is nearing my stop, and I yank the cord. I step out onto the sidewalk. The air is still warm, barely perceptible where it touches my arms. Brandon's car rumbles at the curb, and I open the door and climb in.

I told Brandon about the trial, but I didn't tell him about Nora. I decided not to.

The next morning, I woke up thinking about her, and the morning after that. I allowed myself to do what I hadn't during the trial: I searched for her online. It didn't take long to find her last name, along with a couple of photographs. Her smile was disorienting, like being blindfolded and spun around. I thought of a friend who'd suffered a recent bout of vertigo, how he described that these tiny mineral crystals from one part of his inner ear had wound up in another part, a wrong part, so that when he looked down, they'd roll around and trick his brain into thinking the floor had tilted. Nora's smile did that to me. It located a feeling where it wasn't supposed to be, turned the room on end.

In a book on amateur astronomy, I read that if you can identify Orion and the Big Dipper, you can use them as guideposts to find every major star and constellation visible from the Northern Hemisphere, no matter the season or time of night.

I had found my stars. I had Brandon. I had June. I had love. I had only to redirect my focus, surely that was it: look at them, look at us, look at *me*. I knew who I was in this constellation, beside my two people.

I know how to stop this.

I could interrogate my feelings for Nora into oblivion. But the questions that had once been persuasive seemed useless now. Then,

I'd had the perspective of experience to draw on. I'd had relationships with men, enough to allow me to generalize, extrapolate, connect the dots into shapes. Here I had nothing. I'd never been with a woman. What if the view would be different there—different in ways I couldn't imagine, like the view from a galaxy a billion light-years away? Constellations, after all, are a trick of perspective.

My friend Matthew and I often meet up to work together, and one afternoon at his apartment, I tell him about Nora.

Have you talked to Brandon about this? he asks. He's doing this thing where he talks slowly, pointedly, so serious he almost overdoes it, as though he might burst into tears.

Not yet, I say. I'm kind of afraid to.

I think you have to.

He tells me about his relationship with his wife of twenty-three years, how they talk about their crushes sometimes, how hot the conversations can be. We're talking about different things.

I know, I say. I know there's nothing inherently wrong with a crush. It could be a fun thing, hypothetically, in my marriage. I know this is an option. I could use it as fuel, something to bring home and burn, let both of us feel its heat.

But this isn't that, I say. That's what scares me. I don't want to share this with Brandon.

I invite another friend to lunch. I need to tell someone else, see what another person says.

Have you talked to Brandon? she asks.

I was hoping you'd say something else, I say.

This is normal, you know, she says. I'll bet Brandon will think this is normal too. She reminds me that she dated girls in high school, that she and a female friend hooked up in their early twenties, kissed, shared beds. Now she's married to a man, happily married, with two sons. It's all part of her. It's normal. It's *okay*. She draws out the last syllable, throws her weight into it.

Brandon went to Oberlin College, ran with a crowd of musicians and artists. I remember him marveling once, stupefied, when I told him I'd never kissed a woman. I was the only girl he knew who hadn't. It wasn't that his female friends weren't straight or that they were gay. It was simpler than all that. Even he'd kissed a male friend once, at a party, to try it. It was just fooling around. *Who is the fool here?* I wonder.

A friend's mother has a small vacation house on Bainbridge Island, a ferry ride from Seattle, and we were invited for the Fourth of July. That afternoon, a bunch of us swam out to a diving platform a dozen yards from the shore. The water of the Sound is icy on even the hottest days of summer, and this was the first time I'd ever put my whole body into it, swimming and not just wading. I felt awake for the first time in weeks. Brandon paddled out to us in a kayak, cheering.

At June's naptime, she followed me up the carpeted stairs to a bedroom under the eaves. I lay down with her, still in my swimsuit. It was damp, itchy, but I didn't want to get up. I lay there and thought of a trip with my parents when I was six or seven, a few years older than June. We were in La Jolla, at the beach, and I hated it: the sand, the blaze of the sun, the sunscreen. My mother had a yellow terrycloth cover-up that was styled like a blazer, marigold-colored with thick plastic buttons and shoulder pads, and she gave it to me to put on. I fell asleep in it on the sand. The fabric on the inside was ticklish, its loops of thread rubbing my Coppertoned back like the rough side of a dish sponge. But I liked its weight across my shoulders, a weight that meant protection. I liked the way its warmth was different from the sun's warmth. It was my mother's heat.

Now I curled around my child's sleeping body, her arms soft and solid as water balloons. *Stay*, I said to myself, *stay here. There is nowhere else.*

I wondered where Nora was.

In the bathroom, I peeled off my swimsuit and dragged a comb through my hair. I listened to the voices rising through the ductwork from the kitchen. I'm torturing myself with a hypothetical, I said aloud to no one.

It was a few days later, maybe the eighth of July, 2015, when I told Brandon about Nora. We were lying side by side in bed, on top of the blankets, too hot to get underneath. In the light from my bedside lamp, the wall beyond our feet glowed the color of cooked mushrooms.

I have to talk to you about something, I said. I was looking at the ceiling. He'd been scrolling on his phone, and now he tossed it onto the blanket.

Yeah? he said. Okay.

I'm scared to talk to you about it, I said. My eyes burned.

Okay, he said, more slowly this time.

I've been avoiding it.

It's okay, he said. He was kind.

When I had jury duty, I said, I kept looking at one of the attorneys. This woman in a men's suit. Now I can't stop thinking about her.

Why's that a big deal? he asked. He said it easily, like it really was the first thought that came to his mind. Like he wasn't worried.

It just is.

Why? Nobody's totally straight, right? We're all on a spectrum.

I didn't answer. I had thought I was straight. Straight enough to not think about whether I was straight.

I guess, I said. I don't know. This feels weird.

It's okay.

It doesn't feel okay.

This is normal, he said. You know I've had crushes too.

But this doesn't feel normal. This doesn't feel like that.

Have you even talked to her?

I talked to her a little bit on the last day.

What do you know about her?

Her name is Nora. She's a writer too.

Is that all you know? How do you know you like her?

I don't know. I can't explain it.

Why are you crying? he asked.

I'm so scared. I don't know what's happening to me, I said.

I don't understand why you're scared.

Because I can't stop thinking about her! My voice was rising. I said, It's not going away.

The trial ended barely a week ago, he said.

But I don't like this, I said. I can't stop. I'm making myself miserable.

I turned away, onto my side. Down the street, an engine grunted to life. The left side of my body felt strangely heavy, as though it were sending down tentacles, boring through the bed to the floor.

Do you need to do something about this? he said.

No.

But you've never been with a woman. You never even tried it. Do you need to?

No, I said. I rolled onto my back again, let my fist find the blanket between us. I said, I'm afraid if I do, I'll burn down our marriage.

He made a noise, and then I knew he was crying. It sounded like he was breathing underwater.

I can't, I said.

When I'd imagined this conversation, when I'd played it out in my head, it hadn't gone this way. When I'd conjured up Brandon, I'd gotten him all wrong. *This is the kind of wife you are?* I'd heard him scream. *This is the kind of person you are? We've been married for eight years. We've been together for ten. And* this *is who you turn out to be?* In his place, I would not have been kind.

But he was. Now I'd made him cry, and I knew he was crying not only for himself but also for me. He was crying with me. We were both afraid, of the same thing and of very different things.

Are you going to leave me? he asked.

No, I said, and I believed it.

I don't want you to leave me, he said.

We both cried. I wasn't alone with it anymore: he was with me. We had a shared secret. *We* would carry it, *we* would interrogate it, *we* would outlast it. We.

We lay there, not talking, not fighting. I turned off the lamp, and he rolled to face the wall. I shimmied toward him, slid my arm under his. The smooth skin inside my elbow found the smooth skin of his waist. His skin was like June's.

The

Banana

Painting

2

Brandon and I met in April 2005, the spring that I was twenty-six. He was twenty-three, eleven months out of college, in his first year of graduate school at Brooklyn College. He was a formally trained saxophonist, now getting a master's in music composition. I was in grad school too, for anthropology, and I worked part-time for a university press in downtown Seattle. We were drawn together from the start by a love of food and cooking. I'd been writing a food blog for a few months, and a friend of his told him about it, jokingly playing matchmaker. He read it and sent me an email. He was in New York, and I was in Seattle, but we had credit cards. We'd deal with the consequences later. The first time we kissed was in the kitchen of my apartment, against the closed door of the dishwasher in mid-cycle. Everything whirred.

Food was a hobby that we'd each put to use in short-term jobs and odd gigs to get us through college and after. He'd worked at Pizza Hut, had done some catering, was a server at Balthazar in New York City. I'd also worked for a caterer, and as a restaurant cook, though the stress and pressure of a professional kitchen quickly spun me back out the door. Instead I sold olive oil at a greenmarket and made sandwiches at Whole Foods, reading M. F. K. Fisher like a sacred scroll. The best job I ever had, I told Brandon giddily, was a summer as a cheese monger. He got it.

I'd never felt so perfectly matched. He was smart in all the ways that I wasn't. I knew the lyrics to songs, but he actually knew how to make them. I remember when he played me Nina Simone's "Sinnerman." I'd never heard it before, but I thought right away that he rose to meet the world the same way the song does: light and quick, with an intensity that revealed itself in glimmers, caught me up and made me feel things.

Brandon was easy to like and easy to love. While I was at work, he'd set off on foot or by bus or in my car and find places I'd never heard of. He bought me a funny vintage book about etiquette and a dozen slices of culatello wrapped in aluminum foil. He was a city creature, unintimidated by new places and people. I liked visiting him in New York, letting him lead me around the city. He was a whistler, I discovered. He whistled everywhere he went. Sometimes he even sang, a phrase of Caetano Veloso or Curtis Mayfield. *What I love about New York is that no one cares*, he said, squeezing my hand.

I was quietly crazed with love for him, the way a ceramic bowl is crazed with fine cracks and lines. I felt like I could split open at any moment and it would all spill out, the jelly of my insides, like the alien in a sci-fi movie who looks like a woman but in the act of love is revealed to be a glowing column of light.

He's so *good*, I'd say to friends, catching them up on my news. I wanted to learn from him.

His parents had been hippies, he told me. His mother had given him dolls and trucks, and he'd played soccer and saxophone and taken dance classes. His parents had tried to raise him without gender bias, and as an adolescent, he wanted to join a ballet company one day. I'd never known someone like him.

My mother hoped I'd wind up a gay, ballet-dancing rock star, he laughed. She was disappointed when I turned out to be straight.

Of course, there were things I wasn't sure about. We lived on opposite sides of the country and knew each other in a once-a-month-visit kind of way. He also fantasized frequently about robbing a bank and what he could do with the money. Usually these were altruistic, Robin Hood–y fantasies, which was charming, but they were disturbingly elaborate. It didn't seem very fun to me, daydreaming about something illicit that I didn't want to do. Tomato, tom*ah*to?

Once, visiting his parents in New Jersey, we borrowed their car and went out to dinner. It was late summer, the end of a hot and torpid day, and Brandon half-assed his parallel-parking job. The wheels were three and a half feet from the curb, if not four, and when I suggested that he repark, he scoffed. If I get a ticket, he said, I'll just pay it. I huffed the whole way to the restaurant. We'll never share a bank account, I scolded. I don't want you using my money for a parking ticket you could have avoided.

He had a tendency to talk in absolutes, offering opinions and judgments with an air of immutable fact. He was prone to exaggerations and boasts. I didn't like how big and loud he got, how he stopped listening. I'm from New Jersey! he'd explain. This is how people *are* in Jersey! I bit my lip. I grew up in Oklahoma—what did I know? It was easier to give in.

I couldn't tell what I was supposed to care about and what I was supposed to brush off. I'd dated around, had had one long-term boyfriend. I had enough experience to know that relationships— even romantic ones, *especially* romantic ones—require compromise. But what could, and should, I compromise on? How does anyone know?

I'd seen movies, read magazines and novels and *Cathy* cartoons. I'd heard groups of women talk shit about men—*men always* this, *men always* that—as though men were a unified, homogeneous category, and I'd heard groups of men do the same. It made me queasy. Even people who seemed to be happily partnered talked shit about their significant other in private. How much annoyance with one's partner is normal? A lot of people seem to barely tolerate the person they love. Is that normal? If it *is* normal, is it okay with me, in my life?

Which compromises could I live with and which would fester, rise up between us like a wall? How could I know—and know right now—which attributes were important? What could I live with, for the sake of *us*? How does anyone know? I was happy with Brandon. Was that enough?

The following spring, on a sunny late-March day in Brooklyn, we sat down on a bench beside the East River and he slid suddenly to his knees and pulled out a ring. I said yes and quietly panicked, bewildered and ecstatic, a collision of feelings that felt very sane. We were twenty-four and twenty-seven. We'd been together for eleven months and four days, though we'd lived on opposite coasts for every day of it. We held hands and walked on the waterfront, stopping in a chocolate shop we'd read about. We tossed back and forth dates and locations and daydreams and the question of where we would live. There was another question I remember not saying aloud: *How will we handle our money?* I couldn't make my mouth form the phrase. It was too unsexy, unromantic, anxious. I didn't believe that getting married was supposed to be some blissful state of suspended animation, but I wanted to be elated, swept up, careless. I wanted to be transformed. I wanted to be able to be someone else, even just for a day, maybe a week or two.

Both before and after we were married, I hated the thought of needing someone to "complete" me. Of course I wanted a boyfriend. I wanted to love someone and be loved. But surely I was not lacking on my own, not incomplete. I grew up an only child, so I'd always been on my own, and I liked it.

As I envisioned it, my husband and I would be separate people. We would be as important individually as we were together, as a couple. We'd be discrete entities with our own histories, energy, and motion, but we'd be bound to each other like stars in a constellation: a union born by the force of imagination and emotion, by the curious work of the human mind.

The stars in the night sky are a long way from the surface of the earth, so even the nearest seem to move little, if at all. They appear to be fixed against the firmament from day to day and year to year, permitting us to think them into shapes and symbols. But astronomers know that every star is in motion, that each moves along its own trajectory, according to its own properties. The constellations we see are temporary creations, our effort to draw order and meaning from a mostly unknowable universe, to tell ourselves stories, to guide our way home across oceans.

Marriage is like that too: a method we've devised to protect against the disorder of the outside world, to make sense of the wonderful nonsense that is love. My husband and I would be two individuals who loved and supported and believed in each other, and in so doing, we'd choose to link arms for the long haul.

I don't know if I believe in marriage, I confided to a friend, but I feel somehow that the things we could do together, and the people we could become, will be better than anything we could do on our own. I still believe in that.

We never lived together before we got engaged, not even in the same city, not even on the same coast. It wasn't intentional; it was our chronology. We fell in love and proceeded accordingly. Being together in the literal sense was a foregone conclusion: we'd get there. Brandon happened to propose before we did, because he was excited, because we were in love. The timing was a surprise, but the fact of it wasn't.

Of course now I want to break into the scene, wringing my hands: But did you talk about *kids*? Did you talk about *values*? Did you talk about *money*? Did you sit across from each other and share your visions for life together? Did you make sure those visions aligned, wielding your scrutiny like a carpenter's level? Do you know you could have done that?

Do you think your story would be different?

Brandon finished his master's that spring and was accepted to a doctoral program at the University of Washington. In June, he landed in Seattle for good, and we began searching for a new apartment to rent, someplace that would belong to both of us, a place to start our life together.

We moved into a duplex with passionflower vines climbing the fence out front and furnished it with Brandon's thrift store finds. We sussed out each other's quirks and habits, set rules and aims. Here's one: we decided to never see each other use the toilet. He'd heard somewhere of a couple that had held this boundary, declaring that it protected *the mystery*, some sexual sanctity of our genitals. We both thought it was a compelling idea, and we agreed to try it. When, on occasion, one of us accidentally walked in on the other, the intruding person made a Broadway show of fleeing down the hallway, screaming. That was always fun.

Every night, we cooked and ate together. In September, Brandon started school and, to pay bills, got two teaching gigs on the side. I was still working at the publishing house. I remember when Calvin Trillin's *About Alice* came out that fall, a book-length eulogy to Trillin's late wife. Brandon and I saw ourselves in Calvin and Alice, measured ourselves against their epic proportions.

Trillin wrote: "There was one condolence letter that made me laugh. Naturally, a lot of them made me cry. Some of those, oddly enough, were from people who had never met Alice . . . but they knew how I felt about her. . . . I got a lot of letters like the one from a young woman in New York who wrote that she sometimes looked at her boyfriend and thought, 'But will he love me like Calvin loves Alice?' "[2]

We hung on that passage, reciting it to each other. Did he love me like Calvin loves Alice? Did I love him like Calvin loves Alice? We did. We did, we did, *we did*. We were drunk on it. Our friends teased us for the way we were always touching: foot draped over foot, shoulder against shoulder, or pinkies locked like a pact. I was drawn to his body as though by a magnet. I remember exactly how it felt to slide myself under his arm, fit the front of me to the side of him. We stood that way for years, until at some point, we stopped.

Of course it wasn't like that, and of course it was.

We were both immersed in academia, but neither of us was sold on where it would lead. I was the first to veer off-course, quitting school and working full-time at the publishing house. I wanted to be a writer, and after-hours I wrote a proposal for a book. When I sold it to a publisher in New York, it felt as though the wheels of my adult life had finally found their purchase.

I wrote the manuscript the year that we got married. We hit the ground like thoroughbreds, pacing each other. That fall, as I was finishing the book, Brandon starting toying with the idea of opening a restaurant. We'd made a friend who owned a successful Italian spot in town, and with her mentorship, Brandon began to plan a restaurant of his own: a neighborhood pizza place, Delancey, where he'd make and serve in Seattle the kind of pizza he'd loved in New York.

When he'd conceived Delancey, I'd been so deep in writing that I didn't pay much attention. My whole life had built to this moment: I was writing a book, and it was going to be published! I was learning how to write it as I went along, an intensive process that, many days, left me feeling like my insides had been sucked out with a straw.

I remember conversations about the futility of his doctoral degree, about whether he would go through with it. The degree was important mostly if he wanted to teach, in which case we'd likely have to move to the University of Wherever He Could Get a Job. We wanted to stay in Seattle, but there were few job openings. Having pulled out of a doctoral program myself, I encouraged him to do what felt right. I wanted him to be able to do work he would love, as I now did. Anyway, even if he had the *idea* to open a restaurant, I never imagined he'd do it. This was a man who had, after all, also considered robbing banks. Surely he was no more serious about this than he had been about that. People dream of opening restaurants all the time. I've probably heard a dozen people in a dozen different fields toss out the idea in casual conversation, usually under the influence of a good meal. Most come to their senses. The steps to opening a restaurant are numerous and byzantine, the costs exorbitant, and the failure rate is high. The leap was so large that I assumed he'd never get there.

Brandon liked to dream big dreams. He and our friend Sam even made a game of this type of unbridled thinking. They called it "Think Tank," and it involved taking turns calling out scrappy inventions and lavish solutions to often-dubious "problems." Over a pitcher of beer, they taught me how to play. My proudest invention—in concept, if not in anything near reality—was a potato that would grow out of the ground already cut, fried, and hot, in the style of the Bloomin' Onion at Outback Steakhouse. Big dreams were a fun game.

But while I was writing, Brandon taught himself about building codes and wood-fired ovens, restaurant licensing and leases, how to mix concrete and tile a wall. When I finally came to, when my book was at the printer, I saw that the lease was signed and our basement was impassable for all the scavenged pots and table bases, chairs, and professional kitchen equipment. I understood that I had been terribly wrong. He was going to open a restaurant.

In the linoleum-floored kitchen of our duplex apartment, I sobbed and pleaded. I didn't want a restaurant. I knew what that life looked like—debt, tight margins, long and irregular hours—and I didn't want it. The friend with the successful Italian restaurant had recently filed for divorce. Our relationship stood on a foundation of long dinners and meandering conversations while cooking; now, when I finished my work each day, Brandon would be at the restaurant, beginning his. He would be a chef, working noon to midnight, seven days a week. Opening a restaurant is not a job for newlyweds. I didn't want any of it.

Brandon stared at me blank-faced. His mouth curled, a rictus of disbelief.

The lease is already signed, he cried. I've been working on this for months! His voice had gone high and raspy. I did this for us, he said. I thought you would be happy. Now we can both do what we love to do. That's what I meant this to be. The restaurant will bring together everything we love.

But I don't want it, I said, my pitch rising to match his. It can't be that easy! That's not what this industry is. I tried to slow down, catch my breath. I just never thought you'd get this far, I said. I thought you'd move on. I thought you'd give up.

This would humiliate him, though that wasn't what I wanted. I hadn't believed in him, and now we both knew it.

But I knew whose fault it was. I'd made the huge mistake. I'd been eyeballs-deep in my own work, distracted as I encouraged him in his. I hadn't been clear about what I wanted, or didn't want, because I didn't think I had to be; the restaurant was never, not *actually*, going to open. Now it was.

A friend of mine used to have a phrase taped to the wall of her office: *Accept it as if you'd chosen it.* The first time I read it, it seemed sad. I read it like an admission of defeat, the image of the toddler in the grocery store who, having wailed herself dry on the floor of the cereal aisle, stands and follows her mother in silence to the checkout line.

When we opened Delancey, I saw that I'd missed the point. Accepting it, this thing I had not chosen—this was not defeat but evolution. This was what I'd heard called "resilience." This was sanity.

"Resistance to the unpleasant situation is the root of suffering," intones guru Ram Dass. As a kid I'd seen his name among my mother's books, down at the end of the shelf where she kept *The Dance of Anger* and *Love Is Letting Go of Fear.* Now I knew why she had books with titles like that, whose unnatural collisions of nouns had puzzled me. Here was adulthood: my husband and I owned a restaurant. Love might have to look like letting go of fear. I could try.

Once I'd recovered from the shock and terror that we were, in fact, opening a restaurant, and once Brandon had recovered from his shock and terror at my shock and terror, we began to sort out a plan. With my book now finished, I was between projects, and this lull turned out to be convenient. I could gather up the energy I'd put into arguing against the restaurant and pour it instead into supporting it. I didn't know what to write next, anyway, and it was a relief to not worry about it. I could worry instead about how to help Brandon succeed.

When we got married, we'd each written vows. In mine, I promised to work alongside him to make our hopes and dreams real—a generic sentiment on paper, but when I spoke it aloud, I felt a current pass between us. I knew what this promise meant: that even if I couldn't predict who he would be or what he would dream of, I had bound myself to him.

It occurs to me now that I wasn't worried about myself in this equation, about what *I* might become or want. I was the known quantity, he the variable.

We began to refer to Delancey as *our* restaurant. My first book was published four months before it opened, in April 2009. Between book events, I helped him to finish the buildout, plan the menu, and hire a staff.

When Delancey opened that August, Brandon and I were two of the three cooks, him at the pizza oven and me making salads, starters, and desserts. I was a confident home cook, but in the restaurant, I was anxious and inefficient. I dissolved. A person's got to be on good terms with adrenaline to make it as a professional cook: you've got to *like* the rush, rise to meet it and ride it through to the end of the night. When confronted with a fresh wave of orders, I'd cry, hurling handfuls of romaine punitively into the bowl. Resentment calcified inside me like a bone. After we closed up each night, we'd have to clean the kitchen, because that's part of a cook's job. On our days off, I'd do payroll while Brandon received deliveries. At home, we distracted ourselves with back-to-back episodes of *Battlestar Galactica* and plastic sleeves of sandwich cookies from Trader Joe's.

But I didn't want to leave the restaurant, because I wasn't sure what else to do. And because the restaurant was *ours* now, publicly tied to his name and mine, I didn't want to let go. Brandon convinced me to hire a cook to replace myself and to trim back my work to only admin, the bare tasks of ownership. I liked these tasks, anyway, and it turned out I had a knack for them. I found a place I could accept in the thing I hadn't chosen. And Brandon was right: this restaurant was us, the best parts of us. We got to feed people good food, give them a good night, do work we could be proud of. And it was successful enough that he wanted to open more.

I was in it with him through the heat and chaos of opening. I could pretend this was *our* restaurant, say it like that, even believe it a lot of the time. But I was no restaurant creature. So now I was back at home most days, at Delancey only part-time. I could try to remember who I was, try to figure out what to do next, try to get back to writing.

The house was quiet. I began to cook in our kitchen again. I've never minded cooking only for myself, never needed to be feeding another person in order to justify doing the work. So while Brandon manned the restaurant, I cooked, walked the dog, and started to write a new book, the story of opening Delancey. I started going to therapy to try to make sense of what we'd just lived, and soon I asked Brandon to join me. It helped us, and it helped me.

A couple of nights a week, I'd go to the restaurant for dinner. I sat at the counter, facing the pizza oven, taking in the near-miracle of the place: *We did it.* I was proud of Brandon for opening a business at only twenty-seven and making it into something so good. I was proud of the community it grew and relieved by the money it made. I also knew it wasn't my place. I had to get back to me again.

Did I miss him those nights at home? If I missed him, who exactly was I missing? The husband who'd cooked with me every night, sat at the table with me, played Think Tank with me and Sam over a couple of beers? Or the husband I had now, a chef who was rarely home before midnight?

I'd be flossing my teeth before bed and feel a heavy sensation below my sternum, like something inside me was falling. I was lonely. I wanted to find him in our bed, curl around him like a vine. To miss him felt good and right, because I'd lost something real, our particular way of love. But when he would come home, I was never excited to hear the key turn in the lock. So did I miss him, or not? When he was awake, he stared at the computer or his phone, his head still at the restaurant. He was tired. I fumed, and I also thought, *Look—he's working so hard. Shouldn't you be grateful?*

I traveled often for work and occasionally for pleasure. It seemed normal to me, healthy even, that a person should do things by herself, married or not. When I was a kid, it wasn't unusual for my mother to travel without my father and me. She went to conferences or on trips with her sisters. When my mother was gone, I missed her, but I never read her absence as evidence of a lack of love. I knew she was thoughtful, reasonable, and would come back to us.

"By taking her mind totally off me," wrote the artist Anne Truitt of her mother, "she gave me my own autonomy. . . . I realized that she would have watched me had she not been sure that I was all right. And, if she were sure, I could be sure."[3]

I was proud of my independence, but I did worry sometimes about how little I looked back. I worried at this absence of feeling, the way a child tongues the space where a lost tooth used to be. But I didn't want to be the opposite, did I—someone who never does anything without her spouse? Brandon and I knew couples like that, and we agreed that it didn't suit us. If that kind of dependence would be unhealthy, surely our independence was laudable, a good sign.

Our fights never lasted long. I remember only one night, maybe two, of sleeping on the sofa. But we were not skilled at fighting. We rarely emerged from an argument with a better understanding than we'd had when we started. At some point in any fight, we lost the ability to hear each other, a sort of psychological bursting of the eardrums. Our therapist suggested that when this happens, one of us should rush to the fridge, open the crisper drawer, take out a vegetable, and wave it around. She called this "the eggplant trick" and suggested that the stupidity of it would snap us back to reality. We never tried it.

Every couple fights the same fights over and over, and we too had choruses we'd return to. In an effort to make a life, and to make that life work, we'd assumed particular stances. With him at the restaurant, I did everything at home. When I asked for help, he said I wanted too much. He said I didn't value how hard he was working. If I pointed out a task he'd forgotten to do, he pronounced me petty: If I was the one who noticed these things, why didn't I just take care of it? I developed a habit of collecting discontents, sitting on my complaints and hurts like a clutch of bad eggs. He'd dismiss me as "irrational" or "crazy," which had the logical effect of making me crazy. Once, arguing our way up the steps to our duplex, I pummeled him in the chest with a bundle of mail. Nine weeks pregnant, sitting at our kitchen table as we argued, I lifted a white china bowl of beans over my head and, in the sweaty grip of first-trimester hormones, launched it at the wood floor. It exploded in a confetti of shards and brown goo. I grabbed my keys on the way to the front door and drove loops in the dark while my phone rang, Brandon Brandon Brandon, on the passenger seat.

We had flashes of understanding, moments of seeing our patterns and bad habits. I instated a rule: the words *crazy* and *irrational* were never to be used our house. I could see him sometimes fighting to keep them off his lips. The life we'd built seemed to depend, at least in part, on positions we'd assumed long before, and it seemed impossible, and often inadvisable, to break them.

In early 2011, the *New York Times Book Review* published a rant called "The Problem with Memoirs."[4] I was in the thick of writing *Delancey*, a memoir. The article could be summed up by its snide illustration: the word *Memoir* typed in bold black lettering, marked up by an unseen editor's red pen so that the last four letters were deleted and a period fell after the *e*. The first sentence of the piece was, "A moment of silence, please, for the lost art of shutting up." I shouldn't have read the rest, but I did, and to demonstrate how unfazed—indeed, how *inspired*, how *totally* nondefensive—I was, I printed it out and pinned it to the wall of my office.

There was one line that I highlighted, and I remember it verbatim: "If you still must write a memoir, consider making yourself the least important character in it." I could do that, and I would. I did. I made Brandon the hero of the story and myself the small, miserly villain. *If it's bad form to be the center of my story, then I should be cast out. I must be punished, and I will do it myself.*

We were not a natural team. We were solo artists: he a chef trained as a composer, and me a writer. But we both loved to make things with our brains and our hands, and we learned how to make things together. We got pretty good at it. We made Delancey, and then we decided to have a baby. We bought a house. I wrote books. We created out of ourselves, him and me, things that will outlive us.

We wanted to be kind. We each wanted the other to be happy. We were good at encouraging each other, whether or not we really wanted the outcome in question. I'd vowed to support his dreams, and I never thought it would be simple. His dreams seemed to require so much money, so much risk, such leaps of prophet-like faith, that they excited in me not anticipation but panic, left me grabbing at walls and furniture as though Admiral Boom were about to fire the hourly cannon.

The guy who cuts my hair keeps a note on his mirror: "Those who do too much somewhere do too little elsewhere." I don't know if

Brandon does too much, per se. It's not too much for him. But it was frequently too much for me. He's zooming into some grand future, pinballing from idea to idea and plan to plan. Meanwhile, I'm quietly reveling in making an excellent pot of soup, getting high on the ecstasy of clean sheets. This made us a good match, I thought: his strength fit my weakness, and his weakness fit my strength. We were good at good intentions.

Now we lay on our bed that July night, the summer of jury duty, and I told him about Nora. He listened, and he was kind, and we cried. I saw that it had been a long time since we'd been a *we* this way.

I had not brought him this information as an offering, the way a cat comes in with a dead bird, a tribute in blood. I did not tell him because I hoped to stoke the home fires. I saw in myself the power to burn us down, and I hoped he could stop me, pull me out.

The danger of extramarital relationships, I once read, is that we take them too seriously. I had expected him to be furious. I expected disbelief. Instead he held fast. He accepted what I brought. It's normal to burn sometimes, he said, and he was right. He could soothe me if I let him, and this would pass. I had the power to raze us and the power to choose not to.

The Romantic idea of love—that a person exists who can meet our every need and want—has made much of what we experience in marriage seem horrific and wrong. Philosopher Alain de Botton wrote a much-clicked article about this for the *New York Times*, explaining that most of us "end up lonely and convinced that our union, with its imperfections, is not 'normal.'"[5] Brandon and I had fought plenty over what things we would, and should, consider normal in our marriage. But that July night he didn't fight. He stayed with me, asked me to stay too. I didn't understand what had happened to me in the courtroom, and he didn't either. But he wanted to understand, and I wanted to be understood. Here was something we both wanted. Our secret kept us warm.

In the dark, I pressed the length of my body to his. I had missed him, and here he was.

3

It was a habit now, looking for her. I looked for her on street corners, in the driver's seats of cars as I pulled up alongside. I searched online, cleared my browser history every day, each time swearing I was done. I was a story I'd already heard, tiring even to myself. I could make this go away. Like the welt of a mosquito bite, this itch could only get worse with scratching.

Anyway, the internet gave me little: Nora kept a low profile. I knew almost nothing about her. The more I thought about her, the more stupid I felt. Wanting her contradicted everything about my life, everything and everyone to whom I'd bound myself, and I didn't even *know her*. She was my invention, a pencil sketch from a fever dream that I now pored over for hours, days, weeks. I colored her in with fantasies and fabrications. I made her up.

That fall I enrolled in a fiction-writing class. The first assignment was to read a xeroxed short story whose plot unfolded around a dinner table. To warm up when we arrived for class, the instructor asked us to write for ten minutes about a fantasy meal.

I knew immediately where I would go. I went to Nora's house. I found her in a worn wool sweater at the kitchen table, peeling an apple with a paring knife. The fruit's skin curled onto the table in a single spooling coil.

I'm making pancakes, she said. Thought I might cook some apples in butter.

When I sat down across from her, our knees knocked softly like gloved knuckles. That was as far as I got before time was up. I didn't volunteer to read aloud. My hands had started to sweat.

I don't even like fruit with my pancakes, I thought. A relief.

The instructor gave us a handout on character development. Your characters will have competing desires, she said. That's where stories come from. What your character wants, her internal desires, will conflict with her external reality.

Interview your character, she said, and I wrote it on the back of the handout. *Ask her what she wants.*

To forget about her. That was what I wanted.

We learn in elementary school that a star's gravity keeps its planets in orbit. But planets too have gravity, and as they orbit their star, they tug it back and forth, making the star wobble gently. Our Earth does this to the sun, though weakly; Jupiter, which is bulkier, gives the sun a pretty good yank. The wobbling of stars is, in fact, what allows astronomers to discover and locate planets outside our solar system, planets that orbit other stars. As faraway planets tug their stars to and fro, the light from those stars changes color. As a star moves closer to us, the light waves it emits compress and look bluer; as a star swings away, its light waves stretch, looking redder. A shift in the light of a star points to the presence of an orbiting planet.[6]

Nora exerted this type of gravity, a disorienting pull. I wobbled. But I didn't want to; I wanted to stop. I knew where I was supposed to be, my location inside the constellation of my family. I had to quit thinking about her.

There's a trick for this in meditation: when you catch your mind drifting into thoughts rather than resting in the present, you silently say, "Thinking." Gentle. Easy. No judgment. You recommit to the present.

If I quit thinking about her, my internal desires would align with my external reality. If I quit thinking about her, everything would be like it was before.

My mother moved from Oklahoma City to Seattle that summer, into a house a block from ours. Brandon and I helped her find it, and we couldn't believe our luck, having her so close by. June started preschool that September.

At the class orientation there were two lesbian families. The teacher waved us toward a brown rug at one end of the classroom and asked us to sit. Brandon was home with June, so I was alone, and I took a spot close to one pair of women. I hoped they wouldn't notice the way I planted myself among them. In the child-size space we lowered ourselves to the floor awkwardly, like foals do, the rug too small and our legs too long.

This couple appealed to me. One of the women had floppy light-brown hair that fell across her eyes, tanned skin, glasses, and a gap between her front teeth. She gave a small wave when she said her name, and her fingers were long and slender. Her wife had dark eyes and wavy black hair cut short, tapering along the tendons at the nape of her neck. They wore loose, boxy jeans that frayed at the pockets, what clothing companies like to call "boyfriend jeans." There was evidently no boyfriend.

Brandon and I called them my crushes. He had a crush too, felt a fun little twinge when he saw a particular mom from the classroom across the hall. We joked about it, teased each other. I was euphoric, caffeine-jittery, when I ran into the lesbians at pickup or drop-off. I wanted them to take me in like a stray.

My mother once commented that the black-haired one looked a bit like a boy. I nodded my agreement. I thought, *That's what I like about her*, though I didn't say it out loud.

Not looking for Nora was not working. I noticed girls with short hair and delicate, angular faces, girls whose bodies could pin me down. I noticed butch women, women with graying buzz cuts, women who looked like mechanics, who might sling me over a shoulder. I saw every lesbian and queer couple everywhere. I envied what I imagined they had, their dynamic, their sex.

Was I a lesbian, then? Was that it? Had I been this way all along, and I didn't know it?

Writer Minnie Bruce Pratt was married to a man and had two small sons when she first fell in love with a woman. "Everyone was shocked at the turn I was taking in my life, including me," she writes. "Everyone . . . wanted to know: Had I ever had these feelings before? . . . When had I started to 'change'? . . . I didn't feel 'different,' but was I? (From whom?) Had I changed? (From what?)"[7]

The way I looked at Nora, I'd also looked at Brandon. I remembered it. Was I bisexual? Was that the word for me? *Queer*? My birthday came in mid-September, and I turned thirty-seven. Had this always been in me, like the eggs in my ovaries?

There's a scene in *Fun Home* where Alison Bechdel, then a four- or five-year-old girl, sees a butch dyke walk into a diner wearing dungarees, boots, and a set of keys on her belt loop. It's a powerful moment, young Bechdel seeing a glimpse of who she is and who she wants to be: "Like a traveler in a foreign country who runs into someone from home—someone they've never spoken to, but know by sight—I recognized her with a surge of joy."[8]

I had to have had a moment like this, surely: a flicker of the person I was now becoming. If the evidence was there, I would find it.

4

Early in our dating, Brandon and I sat looking at old photo albums, and a shot of me in college made him laugh out loud.

You looked like a lesbian, he said.

Shit, did I? My hair was now down to my shoulders, but seven years before, when I was nineteen, I'd torn out a magazine photo of a supermodel with a pixie cut and taken it to my hairdresser. There in his strip-mall salon in Oklahoma City, the guy gave it a go. I wore my hair short through college, slicked with pearly goop and mussed into soft spikes. For a while, I dyed swaths of it black or bleach-blond, which made a calico effect with my natural shade of red. I thought this was very punk. Instead, apparently, it looked gay.

The first gay person I knew was my uncle Jerry, the second-oldest of my mother's six siblings. Jerry lived with his partner, Tom, in Santa Rosa, California, in a sunlit single-story house on a property they called Know Creek Ranch. The house was set back from the road by a stand of trees, and at the end of its long gravel driveway sat a barn where Jerry bred Morgan horses and ran a mail-order business selling equine supplies. My mother told me that once, when one of Jerry's horses bit him, he turned around, looked it in the eye, and bit it back. He was soft-spoken and fair, but when my cousins or I would start to whine, he could stop us with a single word. To want his validation was instinctive, obvious.

Jerry had once been married to a woman, and they'd married young. He and his wife lived in Vermont, where she grew up, and had a young son, my cousin Jason. Jason once told me that his mother knew there was something secret in her husband's life, but she was naive enough to not suspect what it was. She was a small-town girl. Jerry was worldly in comparison, having lived in both Vermont and his home state of Maryland. She was blindsided; he was less incredulous. He'd known since his early teens, but he'd hidden it. He figured that if he married a woman, and if he had enough sex with her, he'd grow out of it.

I was born in 1978, four years after Jerry came out. By then he was divorced, and he'd fallen in love with Tom, and they'd moved to California, leaving Jason behind in Vermont. I only ever knew Jerry as one half of Jerry-and-Tom, as a compact man with a runner's build; wavy, rust-colored hair; and a *Magnum, P.I.* mustache. In an album of photographs from Christmas 1979, Tom sits between my grandfather and my uncle Chris, his arms spread wide over the back of the sofa, smiling. In another photo, this one with wrapping paper and coffee mugs in the foreground, I sit on the same sofa, a year old, with my mother in a flannel nightgown on my right and Jerry on my left, my shoulder tucked under his arm. Tom is beside him, chest hair blooming from the open V of his bathrobe.

My parents liked to joke that I was their reward for surviving the adolescence of my half brother. He was the youngest child of my father's first marriage and older than me by fifteen years. By the time I learned to walk, he'd driven a car into a drainage ditch and had been kicked out of high school for an unrelated offense. I came out of the womb eager to please. I got good grades, liked to read and write book reports for fun. I learned to believe that boys are mean when they like you, learned to watch what I ate. I was not discouraged from rocking the boat, but I also was not inclined to rock it more than gently.

When I did act up, my mother's stock warning was mild and even-keeled, and it terrified me: There will be consequences, she said. That was enough, and I would right the ship. I don't remember a time when I got far enough to test her warning; the articulation of it was plenty. Once, at the age of twelve, while playing mini-golf on a vacation somewhere in Colorado, I impishly kicked a family friend's ball off its tee. The adults whooped and applauded because I'd acted my age.

The women of my childhood came in two varieties: doctors' wives and fitness instructors. The doctors' wives wore silk designer blouses and a quantity of makeup that never exceeded "tasteful." The fitness instructors were not their opposite, but close. They were early adopters of Spandex and tanning beds, glowing under halos of body-waved hair.

My mother was both. She code-switched like it was her job, and it was. In aerobics class, she wore a thick brown ponytail that bounced from shoulder to shoulder and an elastic belt that matched her leg warmers. Back home, fresh from a shower, she draped loops of chunky gold Chanel chains around her neck. She'd French-braid her hair while it was still wet, weaving a sleek braid down the back of her head that she'd tuck under itself and secure with bobby pins at her nape. She got her nails done every week, rounded talons coated in red polish, and her lipstick gleamed like fire engines do. She commanded her womanness, shaped it like an arrowhead, sharpened it to a point. She was not just a woman, but *woman-plus*. On a good day, she could have been in a Robert Palmer video. On an average day, she was beautiful, my radiantly eighties upper-middle-class mom.

She stood out in the Bible Belt. My parents were from the East Coast, and they'd met in Baltimore, her hometown. When my father took a job in Oklahoma City in the mid-seventies, they didn't intend the move to be permanent. My mother says she was depressed for the first two years. But they stayed. Eventually they bought a house in Nichols Hills, the ritziest part of town, and sent me to the private prep school nearby. They scoffed at the flat horizon of Oklahoma City, but they also learned how to live with it, how to make the most of it.

Oklahoma is known best for being, in the nineteenth century, the place where the US government put Native Americans it had cruelly expelled from other parts of the country. It is also known for its bizarro Land Rush of 1889, when white settlers raced to grab up parcels of Native land; for the Rodgers and Hammerstein musical of the same (exclamation-pointed) name; and perhaps less so, for having an oil well on the lawn of the state capitol. In the 1980s, if you told someone from somewhere else that you lived in Oklahoma, they'd ask if you rode a cow to school, and this would seem hilarious to everyone but you. But Oklahoma was also a place of new and flashy wealth, and this was especially true in Nichols Hills, a manicured enclave of oil and gas money and gated mansions that people casually called "houses." My father was a radiation oncologist in private practice, and I had a childhood of privilege. My mother stayed home until I was twelve, then made her aerobics habit a job. She became a certified personal fitness trainer. My parents clung to vestiges of their old coastal life: progressive politics and a subscription to the Sunday *New York Times*. We didn't go to church on Sundays. My father instead spent weekend mornings combing estate sales for silver saltcellars, etched crystal glasses, and glazed ceramics from England and France with lobsters and serpents on the lid. He'd hit up the Chinese supermarket, bring home a haul of slender eggplants and crisp-skinned lacquered duck. My parents bought plane tickets and got me out, took me to see other cities and countries.

Nichols Hills was a limited place, a limiting place if you let it be. My parents taught me that, even as they played along. Oklahoma occupies a no-man's-land between the midwest, the south, and the southwest. It has elements of each, but it's none exactly. As it is in the south, though, politeness is king in Oklahoma. You did not talk politics or religion; you smiled first and gossiped later. Nichols Hills had few postcard-worthy vistas, so the beauty you had was everything. People weren't looking out their windows at the mountains or the ocean. They were looking out the window at one another, and at one another's houses. The women of my hometown modeled themselves on the women of Dallas, who modeled themselves on the women of Beverly Hills. My parents half-joked: their worst nightmare was that I would grow up to stay put.

It wasn't until the AIDS crisis that I thought about *gay people* as a category, or at all. I had an out gay uncle in California, but that he was an anomaly in late-seventies and early-eighties America, or in any-era America, wouldn't occur to me until I was in grade school. My parents had told me that some men love men and some women love women, the same way that my parents loved each other. Jerry's being gay was a nonissue within the family.

I know only fragments of the story, of what it took for my family to accept Jerry. My grandmother Elaine was Episcopalian, and her husband, Joe, was a devout Catholic. Their children went to Catholic grade school. But Elaine's parents had been, in her words, broad-minded, and Elaine had a couple of close friends in college who were gay. And Joe, though a quiet, slight man, liked to think for himself. He'd fought in World War II but opposed the Vietnam War and, in the late sixties, wrote a scathing letter to the Archdiocese of Baltimore when the Church refused to take a stand against it. He dictated the letter to my mother, then fresh from secretarial school, and unbeknownst to her and the rest of the family, Joe mailed it not only to the Church but also to the Baltimore *Sun*, where the letter was published for the entire city to read.

Jerry's son, Jason, told me this: that when our grandfather learned that Jerry was gay, and that Jerry's marriage was ending, he took a long, slow breath. Then he stood up from his chair and went to the front door, walked to the local library, and pulled down every book he could find on homosexuality. He read for a while, walked back home, and when he came in the door, he said, Okay.

That was it. In a single afternoon, legend has it, Joe got the information he needed, metabolized it, and accepted it. Now I think, *What the fuck kind of superman does that?* Could this be real—that in the mid-seventies, a Catholic could respond to his son's coming out with not only acceptance but with a desire to be educated, to *understand*? Almost half a century later, it still reads like myth.

Of course it was more complicated: Jerry had a wife and a child, and his coming out would upend their lives. Elaine and Joe did what they could for their daughter-in-law. But they also stood by their son. Jerry joined Dignity, a group of and for gay Catholics, and my grandparents did too. When, several years later, Jerry learned that he had HIV, he asked them to speak at schools about preventing HIV/AIDS. I remember a blurry VHS video of my grandparents in front of a classroom—Joe in brown corduroys and Elaine with her calf-length, elastic-waist denim skirt and a charm bracelet jingling at her wrist—talking to high school kids about their gay son. In my grandmother's files, I found an interview they gave in 1990 to the *National Catholic Reporter*.[9] "People sometimes say to me, 'How wonderful that you treat your homosexual son so well,'" said Elaine. "Well, it's not wonderful at all. It's very easy and natural."

When I was a kid, people would sometimes ask if I was adopted. My parents were brunettes, my dad's hair nearly black. Reddish hair runs on both sides of the family, but my mother always said that I got mine from Jerry. She says I have his nose too, and his freckles. My legs are long like his, the same shape as his, and I walk like he did. When he was already sick, we posed for a picture in the driveway at Know Creek Ranch, nose to identical nose, and you can tell we're saying *cheeeeeeese*.

My cousins and I were once playing at Jerry's house, hiding from the grown-ups, when we found a book about sex for gay men. It was on the shelf above the bed Jerry shared with his partner, Tom, and as soon as we opened it, I knew we shouldn't have. We stared for a minute, maybe not even a minute, before we shoved it back onto the shelf. But my brain held on to those images like I'd studied them for hours. I was probably nine years old, but I can still see them, black-and-whites of tall, hairy men in assorted positions, looking very pleased to be there. I wanted to see more. The feeling scared me, because I hadn't felt it before and because I knew those pictures were not for me. But even as my face burned, I wanted to keep looking.

Around the same time, I noticed a new book in the den of our house. The book was on the shelf where my parents kept art books, and it read ROBERT MAPPLETHORPE in bold gray letters down its white spine. Inside were male nudes with ball gags and leather and elegant, velvety portraits of what I would later recognize as uncircumcised penises. There was a photo of a smirking old lady, the artist Louise Bourgeois, with a giant, ropy-veined statue of a cock tucked under her arm like a clutch. I remember the afternoon that I found it, how I turned the glossy pages with fascination and fear and the strange, slippery sense that adults call arousal. I never told my parents I'd found it. It wasn't that they would have been angry; they'd put it on the shelf, so it was fair game. Making a big thing of it would have only made us all uncomfortable. Still I didn't want to talk about it, didn't want anyone to know how much it confused me.

The year was 1986 or 1987, and by then AIDS was on every front page. I was learning that some people, a lot of people, thought people like my uncle were an abomination. Apparently this was sanctioned by the Bible. Some people thought people like my uncle deserved this new disease, this "gay plague." I began to understand that the way my family understood gayness, and sex, even art, was not how everyone did.

I don't remember how my parents told me that Jerry was sick. The last Christmas that Jerry was alive, the Christmas of 1987, my dad made a video of our holiday. He'd just gotten his first camcorder. We were at my aunt Tina's house in California, and you can hear Mannheim Steamroller's synth-classical Christmas album plinking in the background. The morning after Christmas we drove up to Santa Rosa, to Jerry's house. In the final frames, the camera follows Jerry as he walks up the driveway to the barn. The way his legs work, the sun in his hair like tarnished brass: it really does look like me.

Jerry died of pneumocystis pneumonia on March 6, 1988, in a hospital bed at Johns Hopkins. He was forty-two years old. He'd flown to Baltimore to join up with my grandmother, and they'd planned to travel together to New York, where Jerry would start an experimental drug regimen. But he was sick when he got off the plane in Baltimore, and they never made it.

My mother was forty-one when Jerry died. Her family—Joe, Elaine, the six surviving siblings—tipped from its axis. But in Oklahoma, it was hard to talk about. This is how it was almost everywhere, except

San Francisco, maybe New York, and maybe LA. In many towns, this is how it still is.

But even in towns as conservative as ours, people were dying of AIDS, and local groups sprung up to help them. When Jerry got sick, my mother went to meetings and marches, began to volunteer. The entire family, all across the country, got involved. My aunt Tina was a "buddy" to men with AIDS, driving them to doctor's appointments and caring for them as they died. My cousin Katie made a panel in Jerry's memory for the NAMES Project AIDS Memorial Quilt, and my grandmother made another. Twice, in 1989 and 1992, we traveled—me, my mom, aunts, uncles, grandparents, cousins—to Washington, DC, to volunteer when the Quilt was displayed on the National Mall.

I got white jeans for the occasion. We volunteers all wore white, an army of ghosts walking the tarpaulin pathways between sections of the Quilt. Each morning, we worked as Unfolders, teams of volunteers unfurling the panels over the grass. There was a beautiful ceremony to it, the way we unfolded a square of stitched-together panels, held it taut, and lowered it to the ground. During the unfolding, no one spoke. The length of the Mall was silent, from the Capitol to the Washington Monument. Every panel was the size of a grave; each day, we made and unmade a cemetery.

During viewing hours, we took shifts as Monitors, walking the perimeter of a section of panels, making sure no one harmed or defaced them. I had just turned eleven, but they let me sign up for shifts like anyone else. I had a Swatch watch and a neon-pink fanny pack stocked with Kleenex and granola bars, and the only thing tethering me to my family was the marvelously thin rope of an agreed-upon meeting time. I had an important job to do: me, skinny hips and moussed bangs and too-big teeth, guarding an epidemic's graveyard.

Most of the other volunteers were gay men who'd lost friends and lovers. These men became some of my mother's closest friends. Kids at my school talked about queers, called one another *fags* as an insult. Kids said you could get HIV from the water fountain. I had a black ACT UP sweatshirt with a pink triangle on the front and SILENCE=DEATH written beneath, and I wore it like a challenge, hoping someone would ask me about it. I liked being the know-it-all, explaining that gay people are born gay, the same way I was born with white skin and blue eyes. It's not a choice, I told them. *No one would choose that life.* But back at home, my mother's friends, these beautiful out gay men—they were like celebrities to me.

Those men were my lasting childhood crushes. They were lean and chiseled, well-groomed and well-dressed, and their voices didn't sound like other men's voices. They sounded weird, but in a way I liked: they e.nun.ci.ated, they ar.tic.u.la.ted. They were as heartthrobby as any boy I'd seen on the covers of *Tiger Beat* or *BOP*, and they were *in my living room*. I remember their calves, their white tennis shoes and ankle socks. They were sexy in a way even a preteen girl could understand.

I used to dream about one of them, a dancer in the local ballet company. His hair was the blond of wheat stalks, and he stood with his feet always in first position. He had a smile that made my insides itch. I wondered what it would be like to kiss him. When my parents took me to the ballet, I stared at his headshot in the program and felt my earlobes go hot. I was sure everyone could see them glowing like coals. I couldn't believe my luck: now I had a photo of him to look at whenever I wanted. I had plenty of crushes on boys my own age, but this dancer was a different kind of creature. I knew he was a man, but he was more than that too, better than that, other than that—like there was an extra layer to him, an extra shine. He was, in the words of writer Rebecca Solnit, an "encounter with what else men could be."[10]

I remember another, Michael Freed. Michael had a smooth radio voice, and his cheekbones made a tidy triangle with the point of his chin. He was a working artist, and I tried to copy his style once or twice in art class. My parents had two of his smaller paintings, and they hung them upstairs, where our bedrooms were, among the family photos and framed memorabilia. My parents also had a large painting of Michael's, but they never hung it. It was a banana, goldenrod-yellow and nearly four feet long. The banana was painted against a white background, and along the perimeter of the canvas, under a thin wash of white paint, was a border of old black-and-white photos of boys, high-school-age, in dress shirts and ties. Above the banana was the phrase ONE IN TEN, stenciled in black paint.

That's how many men are thought to be gay,[11] my mother explained. One in ten.

The banana painting was gay pop art. There was no place in our house where it would have fit, or fit in. My parents leaned it carefully against the back wall of a closet, where we saw it whenever we went for the vacuum.

5

When I was thirteen, an older friend gave me a cassette tape of the DC hardcore band Fugazi. When they came through town, my friend's brother, who was older than both of us, took us to the show. One of the singers had a raspy voice that swung between a whine and a growl, and I liked watching him throw his wiry body around. The room was clogged with smoke and smelled like a gymnasium, but I looked around in the dim light at the other girls there. They all looked coolly weird, streetwise, and confident. I wondered how it would be to look like them. I was a straight-A student naturally inclined to a nine o'clock bedtime.

But I could dress like those girls. *Act your way into a feeling*: a phrase from the back cover of one of my mom's self-help books. I got lipstick the color of dried blood and thrifted oversize men's suit pants for fifty cents a pair. I bought a black pleather wallet with a metal chain that I snapped onto one of the belt loops. Nirvana's *Nevermind* came out, and I pulled on opaque black tights under my cutoffs and wore them all winter. I was weird, and I hoped someone would notice. I wanted to be spotted, recognized for being the kind of girl I aspired to be. I knew I was on the right track when one of the doctor's wives grazed me with her eyes and sniffed.

I had to do a research paper in eighth-grade science, and for my topic I chose homosexuality. I wanted to know whether being gay was based in biology. Was there something different about the brains or the genes of gay people like my uncle Jerry, something you could point to that made them gay?

I found newsmagazine headlines that screamed NATURE OR NURTURE? and a couple of studies[12] of gay twins. A group of researchers believed they'd found evidence that the brains of gay men were "feminized" by certain processes in utero. I read about a part of the brain called the suprachiasmatic nucleus, whose size seemed to differ between gay men and straight men.[13] To me this happily proved what I'd been taught by my family, and what I'd been telling the kids at school: gay people are born that way. Sexual orientation is in our biology, went the prevailing assumption: it's an inherent trait, built-in, and consistent over a person's life-span. There's no sense in arguing with it or judging it or trying to change it.

I thought then, and well into adulthood, that each of us has an essential self, and that self is solid, stable, dependable. There would be things I could always count on, like science, and teachers having answers, and the USA having fifty states, and me being me, some elemental *me* that would be constant over my lifetime. Sexual orientation was a part of my essential self.

This made sense to me not only as a person who took comfort in the firm ground of science but also as a kid who wanted vindication for her dead gay uncle. The born-this-way narrative was, and still is, a vital refrain of the LGBTQ+ rights movement. If gayness is something you're born with, like skin color, you have a right to protection by the law. This is also how we talk about transness. Homosexuality was absolved of its classification as a mental illness in 1973, but the rights of LGBTQ+ people still depend on our framing the "condition" as involuntary and fixed.

My mother's artist-friend Michael let me interview him for my research paper, and I called with a list of questions. When did he know he was gay? How did he know? What did his family say? What did he think made a person gay? I remember referring to his "sexual preference," and him gently corrected me: Try using "sexual orientation" instead, he said. We're not talking about who or what a person prefers, because that implies choice. We're talking about who a person is.

I liked boys. That was who I was. It was easy to figure out. In kindergarten, I liked a first-grader named Eli. He was so cute that the sight of him panicked me, as though I'd narrowly missed being hit by a car. One of the teachers at school taught us origami, and I folded love notes into brightly colored swans and dogs. I never talked to Eli, but I invited him to my birthday party that year. He couldn't come, but he and his mother drove to our house to deliver a present. I was in the bathroom when the doorbell rang, and when my mother called to me, I found I couldn't move my feet. I was terrified to see him. I short-circuited, hid behind the bathroom door. I was six. When I opened the wrapped package they'd left, it was just a necklace of ugly plastic beads in primary colors. But I kept it, because he gave it to me.

The next year, in Mrs. Fightmaster's first grade class, I had a crush on a boy named Aaron. My best friend had a crush on him too. He had big earnest eyes and a sweater with his name stitched across it. I didn't even mind when he vomited up his lunch on the rug in front of our cubbies. My friend and I sometimes invited him to climb trees at recess, and when he agreed, I was so excited I could hardly speak.

My mother still remembers her confusion the first time she met a woman with HIV. You just never saw that, she says. Then, as now, gay men were the demographic most affected by HIV and AIDS. The women we met through volunteer work were mostly sisters of men who had died, best friends, or ex-girlfriends. I'm sure some were straight and some were not, but I didn't think about it. My understanding of "gay people" was that they were mostly men.

Gay men packed our living room for support group meetings. I wondered how they had sex, tried to picture it. They fascinated me. One summer vacation in California, I went with my aunt Tina, her husband, and their daughters to the San Francisco Pride Parade, where we saw the Sisters of Perpetual Indulgence drag troupe, their outlandishly made-up faces above dark, flowing habits. On Castro Street, there were men in gold lamé thongs dancing in cages on flatbed trucks. Gay men were thrilling, heartbreaking, tragic, wild. I wanted to be close to them. I wanted them, even though I knew they were not for me.

The idea of being a lesbian seemed boring. Lesbians were less visible than gay men, for one thing. I attributed this to a statistic I'd picked up somewhere, possibly from that conversation with my mother about Michael Freed's one-in-ten banana painting. One in twenty women, the statistic went, is a lesbian. I thought, *That's why we don't know any gay women.* There apparently weren't a lot of them. I remember seeing them on motorcycles at the front of the Pride Parade. They weren't like women I knew. Lesbians were butches. That was how you could tell who was a lesbian. They wore scuffed leather boots, short hair, and lips the color of lips. They weren't pretty. *Why*, I thought, *wouldn't a woman want to make herself beautiful?* "Like most people around me," writes A. K. Summers in *Pregnant Butch*, "I unthinkingly conflated butch with ugly."[14]

In French class, we learned that adjectives follow the noun they modify. *Un sac bleu.* A blue bag. *Des gâteaux délicieux.* Delicious cakes. The only exceptions to this rule are adjectives for beauty, age, goodness, or size, all of which precede their noun. There's a mnemonic device for this, the acronym BAGS. Beauty, Age, Goodness, Size. This is how I learned to understand women, too: in terms of beauty, age, goodness, and size. A pretty woman, a young woman, a good woman, a slender woman.

Lesbians were *woman-minus*. Lesbians were function over form, the Ford Taurus of women. They didn't seem to care about things that motivated the girls and women I knew: about being liked, about approval, about men. They were motivated by something I couldn't understand.

The summer we were sixteen, my cousin Katie and I went to a pre-college program at what was then[15] California College of Arts and Crafts. My mother flew to California with me, and she and her twin sister, Tina, got us settled in the dorms on the school's small Oakland campus. Katie and I were there for three weeks, our first time living on our own like that, without parents. We stocked the fridge with fruited yogurts from Safeway, made peanut butter sandwiches for lunch, and walked down College Avenue to eat black bean soup at a vegetarian place near the Rockridge BART station. I was thrilled by all this freedom, but I didn't feel like testing it. I liked being the kind of kid you could trust to not go off the deep end. We were disciplined, turned in our work on time, didn't drink or smoke. Some afternoons between classes, we'd walk to the Starbucks a few doors down from Safeway and order Frappuccinos. Coming from Oklahoma City, this was the big time.

Each day we had three-hour studio classes in drawing and painting. We drew from live models for the first time. I tried not to giggle or wince as I studied each day's flaccid penis, whorl of pubic hair, or breasts in a variety of shapes. It was much more fun, Katie and I agreed, to draw the female models than the male ones. The male models were hard to look at, all angles or droop, and hairy. The women were softer, more familiar, more beautiful. Katie and I had grown up analyzing, appraising, and envying women's bodies in movies and on the covers of magazines. To study them felt natural.

That summer was the first time I saw a fat woman naked. Our instructor had hired models of all ages and sizes. A couple of the women had thick legs and round, rolling bellies, and I was stunned by how beautiful they were. I had thought they would be ugly. I'd grown up believing that the human body should be—and could be, with sufficient rigor—molded into thinness. *Nothing tastes as good as skinny feels*, the saying went. But these women's bodies, fat and thin and in between, seemed to exist on their own terms—good the way a tree or a flower is good, molecules declaring their presence with the neutrality of fact.

That summer I spent hours lying crosswise on my plastic-coated twin bed, bare feet on the wall, reading Michael Chabon's first novel, *The Mysteries of Pittsburgh*. I'd picked it up for its cover, the title written in loose jewel-toned cursive against a white backdrop, and for the author photo on the back flap, in which beautiful young Chabon appears in pensive black-and-white. His dark hair was gelled swoopily back, and his deep-set eyes were hawklike in their intensity, a sexy hawk. I didn't really understand the book, but I loved it. Like me, I noticed, the narrator watched the world around him from a safe remove. But for one summer, the summer of the story, he somehow managed to get outside himself, to do dumb and impulsive and vitally important things. It was summer where I was too, and I could have done anything, but I didn't know where to start.

That summer I met my first lesbian. Catherine worked for a catering company that my parents sometimes hired for parties. They'd gotten to know the owner of the company, and because I was interested in food, she let me work for a few months in her catering kitchen, doing prep work. The kitchen was out Wilshire Boulevard, one of the main roads through Nichols Hills. But the kitchen was east of all the money, on the part of Wilshire where the mansions gave way to empty shopping strips, warehouses, and arid fields. By mid-June, it got so hot out there that the air above the road trembled like oil in a pan. The lanes were crisscrossed with tar, repairs where the concrete had cracked. When I got out of the car, the hum of cicadas was as loud as the thunderstorms had been in spring.

Catherine was one of two full-time employees, along with a man named Jay. Catherine and Jay bantered like teen siblings. Jay was clever, dry, and quick, but Catherine was truly funny. She was sarcastic and kind. She had smokers' teeth, sinewy arms, and wavy blackish-brown hair cut into a haphazard shag. Her voice sounded like she had a cold. She worked hard and made cooking look easy. She heaved a case of green beans onto the counter and showed me how to snap off their stems and tails. I took it very seriously, as though I could be scolded at any moment, and she laughed at me. It was a pain in her ass to have me in the kitchen, a newbie and a kid, but Catherine was patient. She knew I was clueless, and she seemed to like me anyway. Catherine and Jay held, among other things, a firm belief that the ice cream in a Klondike bar was better than the ice cream in any other frozen confection, and I still find myself repeating that assertion, though I've never formally tested it. They made sure there was always a stash in the walk-in freezer, a treat at the end of the day. I got paid seven dollars an hour *and* I got a Klondike bar.

The fact that Catherine was gay didn't come up much, but she didn't hide it. She never mentioned a partner, and I knew she had no children. I didn't think a lot about it, except to note that her being gay was one more part of her—like her imperfect teeth and her raunchy puns—that made her different from other adult women I knew. Catherine wasn't like my mother or my mother's friends, and she didn't seem to care. I cared, a lot.

It wasn't that I thought my mother lived only for beauty, or for men, or for any prescribed checklist of womanly attributes. But I did think my mother was everything. To me she was an ideal woman: an independent person with her own wants and drives *plus* a devoted mother and wife, *and* she was beautiful. I could see that other women envied her self-possession, her sophistication, that braid-bun hairstyle she made look so easy. It was right that they should envy her. She contained the best possibilities, *all* possibilities, of womanhood. My mother was what life as a woman would, and should, look like.

No one in high school asked me out, and I was afraid to do the asking. It didn't seem valid if I did the work; to mean anything, it had to be the other way around. But I got the feeling that the clock was ticking, that there was an expiration date on my viability as a potential girlfriend. If I didn't get kissed soon, and get my virginity out of the way, then I'd be too old. I liked to read "Dear Abby" and "Ann Landers," and once I came upon a letter that filled me with dread. It was from an anguished thirty-four-year-old virgin. Holding the sheet of newspaper, I had the sense of peering into a crystal ball at my future self.

All my best friends were guys, the best of them being Bobby. He drove a hunter-green convertible with camel-colored interior and wore seersucker suits in the spring. We spent Friday nights drinking chocolate malts from Braum's Ice Cream and Dairy Store and walking the aisles of the Barnes & Noble one parking lot over. When we were eighteen, we drove to Dallas together, six hours round-trip, to buy fake IDs from a guy he'd heard about. I don't think I ever used mine. One day that spring, about a month before graduation, we were hanging out in his bedroom when Bobby said he had a crush on me. I was taken aback. Bobby was my best friend, and the line between friendship and romantic attraction was fuzzy to me. I'd never crossed it before, but I wanted to try. I told him I liked him too, and sitting there at the end of his bed, discussing the idea of *us* like it was a theorem, we decided to give it a try.

We were a stated item for three weeks, but he must have sensed that my heart wasn't in it. He didn't try to hold my hand, and I didn't try to hold his either. Whenever we sat beside each other, alone or with our friends, the many inches of space between our bodies was impossible to miss. The air between us glowed, radiant with discomfort. I felt awful about it, but I didn't know how to fix it. I asked if we could go back to being friends.

One afternoon not long after graduation, one of our mutual friends came to my house to hang out. It was unusual that it was just this friend and me; normally, there were a lot of us. This guy was suave in the way of the stubbled seventeen-year-old poet. He had an acoustic guitar. I had a feeling that afternoon that we were going to kiss, and we did, in the front hall. I was so excited, so thoroughly adrenalized, that my jaw quivered and I bit down hard on his lip. We laughed and kissed again, and then he had to go. Dizzy, half-blind, I reached for the doorknob and missed it by nearly a foot.

That fall I went off to Stanford. Everybody was supposed to fool around in college. I knew this in the abstract, the way you know the earth is round, but I didn't fool around, because I didn't want to. I wanted a boyfriend.

The summer after my freshman year, I stayed on campus and worked in a corn genetics lab in the biology building. I mixed tubes of chemicals to isolate DNA from corn kernels, pipetted liquids into plastic tubes the size of pinky fingers, and whirled them in a centrifuge. The lab had a plot of land at one end of campus where we grew corn for our research and a few other vegetables for fun. We'd have cookouts there each Friday and invite other labs to join us. At one of the cookouts toward the end of summer, I looked up from my plate and accidentally made eye contact with a guy from the visiting lab.

Then, because I could feel him watching, I started looking his way on purpose. I liked catching his eyes on me. He introduced himself: he was a grad student, twenty-six, seven years older than me. The next week we met at the table on the concrete balcony outside my lab and ate our sack lunches together. I was flying to Oklahoma for a visit before classes started again, but I promised to call when I got back.

He was nice-looking, but I wouldn't normally have noticed him. That was no reason not to date him, I reasoned. I'd never "dated" anyone—just that awkward thing with Bobby, and then that kiss with the acoustic-guitar poet—but I figured uncertainty was normal in the early stages of getting to know a guy. Anyway, we can't always be with the most gorgeous person in the room, can we? I thought of adult couples I knew when I was growing up, friends of my mother's and father's. The men often seemed to be sort of mildewing into middle age, while their wives remained taut and youthful. Did those women want their husbands? At some point? Now? Maybe desire was more about personality than looks? I had no idea. But this grad student liked me, and he was kind, attentive, and intelligent. I liked feeling wanted by him.

I emailed from Oklahoma, and the night I got back to campus, he took me to dinner. It was four days after my twentieth birthday. He kissed me, my second-ever kiss. After the next date, we went back to his apartment a few blocks from campus, and I lost my virginity in his twin bed. It hurt less than I'd heard it would—so little, actually, that I asked him: Are you in yet? Afterward, he got up to use the bathroom, and when he came back, his hands smelled like Lubriderm, like my grandmother.

Going on dates, I'd ask myself: *Can I be someone who can live with this?* A ruggedly handsome ecology major who consistently arrives forty-five minutes late and whose sheets are scratchy with soil and dog hair? A blond fitness trainer I met outside a gym who spent our first date talking about his ex and the dreamy daylong bike rides they took together?

I wanted to be fun and low-maintenance, flexible and light on my feet. I wanted to be sleek as a dolphin, able to glide through any situation. I wanted to give everyone a chance. How else would I know what love felt like, if I didn't try?

6

The first time I ate rabbit was with Laura. The meat was shredded and served warm, sauced with olive oil and flecks of cilantro. She'd done the ordering. I'd never eaten rabbit, but I didn't tell her. As I raised my fork to spear a piece, there was a funny beat of wings in my stomach. Next to me, Laura was already chewing, small-talking with the bartender, holding her wineglass by the stem, like someone who knew how to do things.

I was twenty-one, on the cusp of twenty-two. It was the summer after my junior year of college, and I was living at my aunt Tina's house, an hour or so north of Stanford. I worked at Whole Foods in Mill Valley, at the prepared-foods counter, making sandwiches to order and scooping deli salads. Adjacent to prepared foods was the bakery, where I had a crush on a surfer guy who worked behind the pastry case. He had a lean body and hair that fell into his eyes like a horse's forelock. I dreamed about him once: he was in a swimming pool, and he burst through the surface of the water in slow motion, tossing his hair like Sebastian Bach in a Skid Row video.

Across the aisle was the cheese department. Laura was its manager. Her hair was dirty-blond and boy-short, and when she rolled up the sleeves of her white T-shirt, she was River Phoenix in *Stand by Me*. Here was a lesbian. No one said it, but you knew it, the same way you knew she was the boss. Laura was a half-dozen years older than me, not a lot, but she seemed a half-dozen years older than that. She had a way of striding past the cheese case that terrified me. Tough but elegant, stern-faced as an eagle, she surveyed the territory.

This was the same time period that I had my "lesbian" haircut, and it was probably because of that haircut that Laura invited me to a party. We weren't friends, not that I had registered. We'd talked in passing, the way coworkers do, and I always felt afterward like I'd had a run-in with a celebrity: I was honored but incidental. Then one day by the olive bar, Laura turned to me and said, Some friends of mine are having a barbecue this weekend in Tennessee Valley. Wanna come?

The house was off a street I'd driven dozens of times. When I was a kid visiting Tina with my parents, we'd have brunch around the corner at the Dipsea Cafe, drinking our orange juice as we looked over the bay to Tiburon. This time, I hung a left onto Tennessee Valley Road and turned into the driveway of a worn wood-frame house with an overgrown yard that swung toward the street. Inside the house was a small crowd of women in blue jeans and untucked T-shirts, with unmade-up faces that asserted themselves matter-of-factly. They held brown bottles of beer and leaned against the counters. I wondered if anyone there knew that I was not gay. I was at a lesbian barbecue.

Laura's friends welcomed me, and together we set a splintery picnic table in the yard. One of the women was a restaurant cook, and this was her house. They called her Sin, which I later learned was spelled Cyn. Someone told me that Laura was newly out of a long-term relationship. She and her ex had essentially been married, had even had a commitment ceremony on a cliff somewhere, but now Laura's ex was seeing a man. Cyn grilled flank steak and served a corn salad from the latest issue of *Martha Stewart Living*. The salad was so good that I went out and bought the magazine after.

Now it felt like Laura was my friend. We chatted at work. A couple of weeks later, she invited me out to dinner. She chose the restaurant, a new tapas place in Berkeley that I read about in the newspaper. I must have driven to meet Laura at her apartment and then she drove us to dinner, because I remember being in the passenger seat of somebody else's car. The brand-new Sade album *Lovers Rock* spun in the CD player. I wondered if this was a date.

It was still daylight when we got to the restaurant. Laura knew someone there, and they put us at the bar. We must have talked, had things to talk about. I pushed my shins against the patchwork tile in front of our chairs. My palm was sticky on the lip of the bar, and I pressed my sternum into my knuckles.

I watched Laura as she talked to the bartender. Her voice was gentle but gravelly, like extra-fine sandpaper. She had a late-summer tan, and her eyes were opaque as a pot of brown shoe polish. She didn't seem to care that she looked like a boy, like a lesbian. Her mouth smirked a little, even when it was relaxed. It was a good smirk.

Who is she? A weird feeling rose in me. I wanted to put my face close to her, close enough to smell her. I wasn't sure if I thought she was cute or hot or any word I could find, but I wanted to touch my cheek to her cheek, graze the fine blond hairs on her earlobe. I wanted to glide my nose like a cat along the line where her T-shirt met her neck.

I was aware that Laura was a woman, and that this made her different to me, in that moment, from a man. I was aware enough to be scared of what I felt. I was aware that I wanted to kiss her and that I could not imagine getting involved with her vagina.

What kept me from imagining sex with her? I had never cringed at the word *vagina*. But I was still a product of a world where what's between a woman's legs was only fathomable in its relation to a penis. Did I think Laura would feel lumpy or slimy, gross? Did I think I'd find something alien inside her, like one of Carolee Schneemann's paper scrolls? Or was it something else? Did I shy away for the same reasons that I felt unsure of myself with men? I'd had sex for the first time at twenty, an age that seemed embarrassingly old. I was still getting my footing as a bona fide Sexually Active Person. I was timid, must have been spastic as a filly. But at least with men there was a script to be had. I knew what it looked like, what it felt like, what it was to be a woman wanting a man. I had no script for wanting a woman.

Laura drove us back to her apartment and showed me around. The kitchen looked like a grown-up's, with handmade ceramic bowls and tall mullioned windows that wrapped around a corner. She'd lived there with her ex. In the living room, we sat down—me on the sofa, Laura on a chair. I still didn't know what this was, but I wanted to kiss her. I felt suddenly brave, like someone else.

I don't know how to say this, I tried, but I'm really attracted to you. I couldn't read her face, so I kept going. I've never been attracted to a woman before, I said. I've always thought I was straight.

She must have said something in response, but what I saw was her watching me. Everything else went blank. She must have told me she couldn't, or she wouldn't. She didn't touch me. Nothing happened, and I went home.

If it was a date, and it seemed like one, why hadn't Laura wanted to kiss me? I'd done something wrong, though I wasn't sure what or to whom. I'd been stupid. Even if it was a date, of course she didn't want me once I'd admitted my inexperience, my confusion. She was on the rebound, didn't need a project: a brand-new, straight-off-the-lot baby dyke. She'd shut me down accordingly.

Still I liked the idea of Laura wanting me, though I wasn't sure if I liked that I liked it. This was harder to parse. I couldn't imagine dating her, or any sort of ongoing thing, a relationship. It had been a leap to imagine anything, to sit at the bar next to her and understand that I wanted to kiss her. In that moment I'd been there and also not there: a version of me had hovered near the ceiling, watching, wondering which was the "real" me. Was I the person in the chair down there, or was I this one, up here? How would I know? Then the minute had passed, and I'd floated back down to my seat. I'd stayed. I rode in Laura's car, I sat on her sofa, I told her what I wanted. I became someone who surprised me, someone interesting. And then nothing happened.

Nothing happened, but I felt bigger somehow. That I could be attracted to a woman, this woman, the way I was to men—the knowledge of this made me feel larger, my body capable of pulling in more air. I had imagined it would feel different to want a woman, different from wanting a man, but it didn't. It felt expansive. *Expansive*, a word I couldn't remember ever using, now instinctively in my mouth.

But alongside this feeling came another: I was relieved. I was relieved that nothing had happened, that the decision had been made for me. The thing was out of my hands. *At least I won't have to tell my parents I'm a lesbian.*

Summer dwindled into fall, and I moved back to campus. I thought about Laura for a few weeks. Thanksgiving came, and I spent the long weekend at Tina's house. I went to the store, but Laura was gone, had taken a new job elsewhere. I didn't reach out, though sometimes I wanted to. I was taking a medical anthropology class that quarter, and there was a boy who usually sat in the row ahead of me, with auburn hair and cheekbones like twin mesas. I had a crush. It was fun, like it always was.

The next summer I worked again at Whole Foods, this time in the cheese department, Laura's old domain. The manager now was a soft-spoken man who'd spent some years living in Spain. He taught me how to pronounce the Basque cheese Idiazábal, letting my tongue glance off my front teeth, turning the *z* into a *th*. It was a different summer, less fraught. I didn't look at a woman again the way I'd looked at Laura. I didn't even think to look at a woman that way for fifteen years, until the morning I walked into the courtroom.

So what was it? Was I gay all along, or bi, and I'd just looked the other way? After nothing happened with Laura, hadn't I been a little glad? Of course: that must have been when I went into the closet. People don't just *become* gay. I must have repressed it, buried it so deep that even I couldn't find it. As a child, I'd never believed what I heard other kids say about gay people going to hell. But the fact that people said it left a mark. It raised a fear, a prickly, painful thing, a splinter for other fears to snag on. I didn't want to be gay. I thought, *Who on earth would want to be gay?* Though I knew that other people's hatred was wrong, the splinter must have dug in fast, so deep I couldn't see it. I felt a low humming relief, when I understood what it was to be gay, that I was not that.

Early on in dating Brandon, when we swapped dating histories and have-you-evers, I'd told him about Laura, about how confusing and exciting it was, how sad and strange. It was no big deal for either of us: *People are complicated, ha-ha!* Now we'd been married for nearly a decade. Now I wanted Nora. All that time, had this been under the surface, waiting to surge up like magma, frothy and fast, solidifying where it met the air? If sexual orientation is something you're born with, I must have always been gay, or bi, or whatever I was.

But I'd thought being closeted meant, at the very least, that you knew what you were. That made sense to me: you hid because you had something to hide. I'd never felt I had anything to hide. I had felt straight, with one strange exception that never went anywhere. Laura had confused me because she was an anomaly. But once the confusion and the wanting subsided, I didn't feel *not*-straight. I felt like there was simply something about her, an isolated case. Even after Laura, I knew my story. My story made sense.

Is there another universe where the story could have gone otherwise? How good is my imagination?

The summer after college graduation, I went home. My dad gave me a job at his office, combing through old patient files and compiling data on colorectal cancer that I doubt he ever planned to use. I was glad for the cash and the time to figure out what to do next. One weekend my mother and I drove up to Tulsa to visit a friend. In a grocery store there I recognized the cashier's face: it was Aaron, my first-grade classmate, the cute one who'd puked by the cubbies. He'd switched schools when we were eight, and I'd lost track of him. Now he too was a recent college grad and a music writer for the local newspaper, and he also worked a checkout line at Wild Oats Market. There was a tiny silver hoop in his nose, and his hair was dyed black, a shaggy halo around his face. But his eyes were still big and serious, and as he rang up my bag of bulk-bin granola, it somehow came out that we were both reading *The Fountainhead*. Emboldened by the coincidence, I called information and got his number.

The first time we had sex, I hovered over his face and, with what I hoped was a seductive wink, said: What would our first-grade teacher think if she saw us now? I felt like I'd won a prize I'd trained years for. We fell in love fast and thought little of driving ninety miles of highway to be together. He lived in an apartment with a friend and two electric guitars in a building that backed up to a small, fragrant pond. We liked to sit out there and talk late into the night. We lay on the mattress on his bedroom floor, listening to Sleater-Kinney. Sometimes when we kissed, we'd pause by some silent agreement, our lips millimeters apart, and hover there, breathing in our shared heat.

We were together for three years. For two of them, we lived in different cities. At first Aaron was in Tulsa, and I was in Oklahoma City. Then I packed up and went to Paris for nine months, to take a job teaching English conversation. While I was there, I applied to graduate schools, and Aaron applied to Teach for America. Then I moved to Seattle to start school, and he moved to Mississippi, where he'd been posted. He joined me in Seattle the following year, which turned out to be our last. It was difficult, for reasons mostly out of our control. My father had just died of cancer.

The diagnosis came the week that I started graduate school, and my father would die ten weeks after. I took a leave of absence and went home for most of those weeks. I'd grown up around death: first my uncle Jerry died of AIDS, and then, fifteen months later, my mother's younger sister died of cancer. Then my grandfather Joe passed away, and then an aunt by marriage. This was all before I was out of my teens. But my father's death was the first time I felt grief inside my own skin. I didn't know what to do with it, how to keep from bursting open as I watched my father's body fail on a rented hospital bed in the living room. I remember going into the kitchen one afternoon and hoisting myself onto the counter. I sat there and stared out the window at his unused car in the driveway. I started to cry, and then I cried so hard that my hands went numb, and then my arms too. Family friends were supposed to be coming over for a visit. I heard the doorbell ring, but I couldn't stop. The house echoed with my strange, croaking sobs. My mother appeared at some point, eased me off the counter, and wrapped me in a coat. One of my cousins was with us that week, and my mother handed her the car keys and pointed us out the side door. My cousin drove me around, around and around the neighborhood, until I could breathe again. A few nights later we stood at my father's bed, rubbing his knobby knees through the blankets, and watched him leave.

Back in Seattle, I tried to stay the course. I reenrolled in school. Aaron moved in, and we were elated. But living together opened up cracks in our relationship. My grief was a third person in the bed. It was exhausting and sad.

7

When Brandon and I met a couple of years later, everything felt so good, so easy, so unlike anything that came before. Everything was possible. *Can I be someone who can live with this?* Yes, I can.

Brandon and I talked sometimes about having kids. He loved children, had grown up with two sisters and many cousins, and he'd always imagined himself as a father, maybe even a stay-at-home dad. I was undecided. I'd never been able to see myself as a mother, had never wanted it. He'd known where I stood from the beginning, and it had never been a sticking point. Nothing was decided. There was plenty of time, and there was so much else to our lives: I was a writer, and he was a chef, and we had a restaurant. Nothing was obviously missing.

I was only a kid when I noticed that other girls and women seemed to love babies, couldn't wait to get their hands on them. I envied what seemed like their natural desire to nurture, to love, to care for. I also scorned it. I didn't want to be like that, to play the role women are expected to play. I wanted it even less when I thought about the physical reality of birthing a baby, of pushing a human out of the small hole between my legs. The prospect of doing that with my own body seemed as unlikely as growing a tail.

This feeling was reinforced by the fact that my periods were irregular, sometimes nonexistent. My parents took me to a gynecologist, an endocrinologist, a naturopath, another endocrinologist. I didn't ovulate consistently, they found. At nineteen, to regulate my cycle, I was put on the Pill, and because it worked, I stayed on it. I believed this all to be a sign, though I wasn't sure from whom. I would not become a mother. My body was broken.

Still, I did wonder: What would my mother's life have looked like without me? My love for her was so natural, so clear, that I couldn't imagine not having something like it in my own lifetime. I couldn't imagine having children, and I couldn't imagine life without them.

The spring that I was thirty-two, a friend came to visit. She was pregnant with her first child. One night when Brandon didn't have to cook at the restaurant, we made dinner for her. At some point, the topic came up, and we told her our qualms about parenthood.

Surely you know, our friend said, looking pointedly at me, that your irregular period is not some sign from the universe. It doesn't mean anything. Don't let that be the deciding factor.

I don't know, I said. I'm scared I won't like being a mother. I'm scared of giving birth.

Of course you are, she said. Having a baby, becoming parents—these are totally reasonable things to be worried about.

How did you decide to do it? I asked. It doesn't seem like you're worried.

Of course I am, she said. Everybody's scared.

It just seems like the wrong time, Brandon said, and I nodded. We'd been married for four years, and Delancey had been open for not quite two.

There's never going to be a good time, our friend said.

Something about it stuck. A couple of days later, Brandon and I rehashed the conversation. The terrain had shifted. The fear was still there, but it felt manageable, even reassuring. We were cautious because we were taking parenthood seriously.

We decided to try. I assumed we'd have to go straight to a specialist, but I offered to call our regular doctor first, the family physician who saw both of us, and ask what to do.

The doctor laughed merrily. Have you gone off the Pill? he asked. That's the first step.

But I don't get a period without the Pill, I said. I don't ovulate.

Just try it, he said. Let's not jump to conclusions. Give your body a few months off the Pill, and we'll see what happens.

My period arrived the next month. When I saw the bloody toilet paper, I yelped with surprise and scream-laughed. I wanted to run through the house waving it over my head. I was pregnant six months later. For all my difficulty imagining becoming a mother, pregnancy was easy on me. My abdomen stretched until it was round and tight, smooth as a ladybug. I couldn't get over the fact that my skin could stretch like that, *that* far. Thinking about it gave me a deep, shivery kind of pleasure, like the first sip of a strong cocktail. I quietly cheered: my body was made for this. I'd had my doubts, but here we were.

I was nine weeks pregnant when my mother called with news: my aunt Tina, my mother's twin sister, had been admitted to the hospital. She'd been having stomach pain for a few weeks, and more recently nausea and vomiting. A couple of days later we'd learn what it was: late-stage pancreatic cancer. She was sixty-five and looking forward to retirement, had recently bought herself a new white bicycle with upright handlebars.

Tina couldn't go back to her house, where there was no one to care for her, so my mother helped her fly to Oklahoma. Tina's daughters and I rotated through town to help care for her. We had been through this before, too many times. We knew how to talk to doctors and nurses and how to speak the language of palliative care. But there was something about those weeks with Tina that I couldn't penetrate. It felt wrong to be making life while Tina was leaving it. She couldn't eat, and I was hungry. I kept a jar of peanut butter in my tote bag with a loaf of bread whose plastic wrapper crinkled as I walked down the hospital corridors. In a bathroom with fluorescent lights and a folding seat in the shower, I took photos of my pregnant belly.

Tina died at my mother's house, in a rented hospital bed like my father. The night before she died, my cousins slept on the floor beside her bed. It was early morning when her breathing changed, when they called for my mother and me. I stroked her hair, streaked silver at the temples, long and wiry like my mother's. Their hair had always reminded me of horses' manes, the strands coarse and distinct. I was twenty-five weeks pregnant that morning. As I leaned over Tina's body, the aluminum rails of her bed left pink stripes across my tightening belly.

I was supposed to be writing. I got pregnant in the early stages of writing my second book, *Delancey*. Then Tina got sick. Then the shop next door to Delancey moved out, and Brandon leapt at the chance to take over its lease and build a bar there. I did not leap with him. I didn't want another business. But I also knew that, poor timing aside, the bar would probably turn out to be a smart business decision. I let him leap. He worked at Delancey by night and on plans for the bar, to be called Essex, during the day. With six weeks until my due date, I finished the manuscript. Three weeks later, he opened Essex. Three weeks after that, on September 9, 2012, I gave birth to our daughter, June. We closed Delancey and Essex for two weeks, so that Brandon could stay home with us. Then we reopened, as if nothing had happened.

Sometimes I hear myself tell people that our marriage was pretty ordinary. It was happy and unhappy in ordinary ways. Ours is the story of a set of circumstances that were tolerable in isolation, that felt normal and reasonable as we encountered them. It was only with time, and accumulation, that they became intolerable. It was okay until it wasn't.

I don't remember much about opening Essex. I remember that the Japanese anemones in our yard had started to bloom, pink and droopily cheerful, their heads swaying on thin necks in the breeze. That was the year that I learned their name. I'd never cared about flowers, but this was different. Here was a flower that bloomed in time with our baby.

No, I don't remember much about opening Essex. The opportunity arose and was taken. A business-owner friend who already had children gave Brandon some advice: Open Essex before the baby comes, he said, even if you've got to rush. The idea was that after the baby was born, we wouldn't be able to get anything done for months, and then we'd be paying rent on unused space. So Brandon rushed. The whole process happened in four months, start to finish. Then we had two businesses and a baby. There are ways of living that you can live with, until you can't.

Can I be someone who can live with this?

A quieter corollary: *Who is that someone?*

Who was I, to ask for something other than everything I'd been given?

Sometimes I hear myself say that Brandon and I always had the same big-picture vision for our lives, the same end goal. We just had different ideas about how to get there. We had different maps to the same destination. But, writes Annie Dillard, "how we spend our days is, of course, how we spend our lives. What we do with this hour, and that one, is what we are doing."[16] Did we really want the same thing at all?

In the final pages of *Delancey*, I wrote, "I see now that Delancey was the beginning of a process that will continue to shape, stretch, and reshape us. I don't know what we would be without it, that process, that constant growing, but it doesn't mean that I crave it the way Brandon does, or that I always like it. But I've learned now that we can withstand it, and that I can withstand it. I consider it a great personal victory that I could be eight months pregnant, helping to pick out crown molding for a bar that, for all I knew, could open on the same day that I went into labor, and not have to breathe into a paper bag."

I would not revise this assessment. But I would add something now: that one cannot live at one's limits for long. One cannot stay there indefinitely, not even for love.

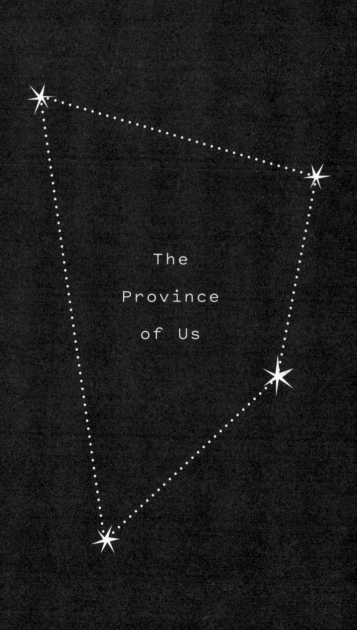

The

Province

of Us

8

On *Fresh Air*, I listened to Terry Gross interview therapist Esther Perel.[17]

Gross: So you say sometimes when we seek the gaze of another it isn't our partner we're turning away from, but the person we've become. We're looking for another version of ourselves. Can you expand on that for us?

Perel: When you pick a partner, you pick a story. And that story becomes the life you live and the parts of you that become expressed. And sometimes you realize after years of living those parts of you that there are other parts of you that have virtually disappeared.

The summer of jury duty, I felt close to Brandon. When I told him about Nora, I'd made us both afraid, but we were afraid together. We talked about it, unpacked it, worked at it. We had sex more often than we had in years. We carried the fear between us like an open secret.

That fall, 2015, June turned three. We were managing, like parents of young children do. We had about a dozen hours of paid childcare a week, a regular schedule we'd worked out with a young dancer who bussed tables at Delancey and babysat on the side. I didn't have enough work to justify spending more on childcare. I was once again between writing projects, between ideas. Meanwhile Brandon got a new opportunity: a third restaurant on a busy corner, a lucrative idea he wanted to call Dino's. I got angry. He knew I didn't want another business, but he tried to convince me anyway. I let him convince me. I didn't stop him. The location was too good to pass up, he said. And in some ways, Dino's would make Delancey and Essex easier to run, because *economies of scale!* This was all good reasoning. But another restaurant was also another siphon on our hours, days, months, attention. I didn't want it. I wished we weren't having the conversation. I wished what we had was enough.

Building restaurants is a twenty-four-hour work cycle. I was used to periods like this, but now we also had June. I didn't want to help open Dino's. I would make a different contribution to the family business: I would pick up the slack at home, doing more parenting while Brandon worked extra. That I could do. I would protect myself and June from the chaos of opening a business. But soon I felt stuck: How would I ever be more than the primary parent for our child? He said I was being dramatic, and I knew I was. The restaurant would open, and then we'd find a new rhythm, a new normal.

But a question: If this is what lots of marriages look like after children—if this is "normal," as we're told it is—does that mean it's okay?

No, this question instead: Is it okay with *me*?

It was okay until it wasn't. I was angry, and I was often on my own with a three-year-old. When I wasn't with June, I was with the contents of my skull. I thought of Nora. I thought of the lesbian mothers at June's school, and every other lesbian-looking woman I saw. The fear that I'd planted that summer in our marriage, I watered it. *I* was what we were afraid of. I was the one who'd brought this into our house, the credible fear of our undoing. I should be the one to rout it out.

That fall and early winter, I devoted myself to the task. I tried to go back to who I'd been before jury duty, to unsee whatever I'd seen in Nora, unfeel what I'd felt. As the months went by, I did manage to stop thinking about her. Thinking about her made me feel crazy, because it had no basis in anything. It *was* crazy. So I willed myself to stop, and after a while, it worked. I broke the habit.

But the ground did not resolidify. It was porous now, and fertile. I watched my desire spread like seeds on a stiff wind, stick to women in coffee shops and on the street and outside school. The seeds bloomed, proliferated like invasives.

June was in school each morning from eight forty-five to eleven forty-five. Sometimes after pickup we'd go visit Brandon at Dino's, and the three of us would have lunch. The place was progressing nicely. It no longer looked like the check-cashing business it had been, with bulletproof glass and a burgundy laminate counter that curled like a question mark. Now the counter was gone and the drop ceiling too, along with the stink of cigarettes that had infused both. In their place was the sweet-sour perfume of sawdust and an airy, tall-ceilinged room trimmed with painter's tape. There was reason to be proud.

I have a picture of June at Dino's from around that time, before the bar and the booths were built. A square of white light falls from the high windows, and June sits on the floor where it lands, perched on the edge of a two-by-four, with the doll she calls Big Baby. She's wearing a pair of grape-purple Puma high-tops with Velcro straps, and she's looking somewhere above the camera, eyebrows a little up, mouth pursed, like she's about to say something. She looks like a doll herself. The photo was taken by a friend who'd been visiting town with her husband. A few weeks later, my friend called with unexpected news: she and her husband had separated. When I look at the photo now, in one of the albums I keep for June, it too seems like a picture of a marriage that's ending.

9

We went to see family for Christmas, and when we got home, rather than thrill as I usually did at being back in our own bed, I felt like I had disappeared en route. Everything and everyone seemed far away. It had been seven months since jury duty, and I had never lost count. I felt worse, not better. To hide from the shame—or was it to escape everything else? To give in to the fantasies?—I tunneled under, sunk even further into my head. I told no one what I was thinking.

A friend was having a big birthday at the end of January, and he invited a bunch of us to a rental cabin in the snow. Brandon took the weekend off, and to celebrate the occasion, we bought new winter gloves, hats, and snow pants. For June, I brought along a brand-new copy of Candy Land, my favorite board game as a child. I had grand visions of us playing it, visions that evaporated as soon as I set it up, when I remembered it's an instant nap for anyone over age ten and June was enraged that it had rules.

Instead, we rented cross-country skis. The first afternoon, even June made it a few yards. Then a friend took her back to the cabin, and the two of us got to ski on our own for a while, on a path through the woods. I hadn't been on skis since I was a kid, and I'd forgotten how quiet it was, the smooth and efficient swish of polyethylene through groomed tracks. We'd needed this, to move together through the cold winter air. Our noses ran, and we licked our lips and wiped them on our sleeves.

In the cabin, the heat vent was too close to the bed. I couldn't sleep, so I watched my husband and our child, these people I called mine, sweat sticking their twin hair to their twin faces. I put on my headlamp and boots and shuffled to the outhouse. Orion glittered above the tree line.

On the drive home, I rode in the back with June. Snow was falling through the bluish dusk. June asked me for a story about Olaf, a friendly giant I'd made up who often got into scrapes requiring the help of his human friend June. As I spoke, she nodded off, and I caught Brandon's eye in the rearview mirror. I told him about a thing I'd recently heard her say, that she'd pointed at her own belly and said there was a baby there. She wanted to call the baby Juicebox. We laughed, wheezing, not wanting to wake her.

How could this kind of contentment coexist with the mess in my head? How could this love coexist with the desire for a whole other love? Shouldn't they cancel each other out? I had watched my husband and child sleep, choked with feeling. I wanted to press a woman against a wall with the length of my body, a woman who looks like a boy, and fuck her. Does one life preclude another?

I wanted both, two lives in this body, running alongside each other in parallel, like ski tracks.

I get email newsletters from the Gottman Institute, famous for its research on relationships and marriage. The subject line of one reads, *Move from* me *to* we.

"It's important to move from *me* to *we* in your marriage," the email says. "What do we need? What do we want? What do we like? . . . You get the feeling they are 'in this together.'"

This struck me as a noble way to operate. Very country-above-self, one-nation-under-marriage. I wanted to stand under that flag. But I had mixed feelings when I heard or saw it in practice, the sort-of royal we. *Oh god, have you seen that new Wes Anderson movie? We hated it!*

Was there a time when I thought of Brandon and me that way, as a unit that moved and thought together? If I had, it was with effort, not instinct. This felt like a personal failing. Brandon and I talked about it, attributed it to my being an only child, screwed from the get-go. The bridge between the poles of *we* and *me* felt perilous, like a slackline over a pit of snakes. I knew I shouldn't linger; for my own safety, I should choose one or the other.

Now that we were people who skied, we decided to do it again. This time we'd leave June with my mother, and that would be nice, a day-date. It was February, and Brandon was working every day, doubles on the weekends. But on President's Day there'd be no construction work at Dino's, so Brandon could take the day off. We'd drive an hour east, over Snoqualmie Pass, and ski for the day.

I knew this had to be it: I should tell him what I was feeling. In the passenger seat, I practiced opening my mouth, forming syllables like smoke rings.

There's something I want to talk about, I said. I've been feeling really down. Maybe you could tell.

You've seemed off, even when we were at the cabin, Brandon said. He glanced over at me.

You remember how I felt last summer, after jury duty? I can't seem to make it go away.

You mean how you felt about that lawyer? he asked.

Not just her. I sort of talked myself out of thinking about her. It made me feel nuts. But now I keep noticing other women.

The lesbian moms at June's school?

Yeah, I said. I can't stop thinking about it. Remember when you asked me last summer if I had to do something about this?

You mean hook up with a woman? Brandon asked.

Yeah. But I don't want to be with a woman like me—not, like, a straight married woman who's just "curious."

What do you mean?

I want to know what it's like to be with a woman who loves women. It just—it doesn't interest me otherwise. I paused, trying to decide if I should say it, and then I did: I want to know what it's like to be with a lesbian.

I don't know how I feel about that, he said. That seems really different.

I stared at the dashboard.

What if you fall in love? he said. Isn't that what you're saying you want?

Am I? Surely I don't want actual love?

I don't want to fall in love, I said. I don't plan to fall in love. That's not what I want.

Because I really don't think it's okay to fall in love with someone else, he said.

That's not what I'm talking about. I just said that.

But what if it happens? he asked.

I mean, I hope it doesn't. It doesn't have to. I paused, considering. Then I said, But I think, you know, being with someone else—maybe even falling in love with someone else—doesn't have to change my love for you.

I don't think it's right to fall in love with someone else, he said.

I didn't reply.

So we would open up our marriage, he said.

Yeah, I think so.

I really don't think it's okay to fall in love, he said.

You don't have to, I said. We get to decide what this looks like. We get to choose. We could buy some books about open relationships and read them together. I've been looking up stuff online.

I don't know, he said. I don't know.

You can date other people too, I said.

I mean, I know how dumb monogamy is, he said. But I never expected you to be the one to want an open marriage.

I know. Me neither.

I think I would feel okay if you only dated women, he said. No other men.

I don't want to date other men.

We watched the road for a few minutes, not saying anything.

I don't want you to fall in love with someone else, he said.

Let's buy some books about this, I repeated. We can learn about it and talk. Set some rules.

But is this something that's true, that's real? he asked. Like, you actually just want to explore this? Or is this an excuse to leave me?

The road was climbing now; we were nearly at the pass.

I'm open to trying this if it's really what you say it is, he said. But not if it's an excuse to ease yourself out the door.

I mean what I say, I said. I'm not going anywhere.

10

During our engagement, before we were married, Brandon and I both had dreams about being hit on by others. I remember feeling horrified by my suitor's advances, thrusting out my hand and yelling, "STOP! I'M MARRIED!" In the morning we'd laugh about it.

I did not want to cheat, not then and not now. Whatever this was, it would not be that. What I wanted was a work-around, a pass. I wanted a pass to be with a woman. Brandon too would have a pass.

This would not be a threesome, not a fun kink to "spice things up." This would be separate from us—cordoned off, but permitted. I didn't want to hide it from him. Isn't that what cheating is: Something you hide, because you're breaking the rules? Then let's rewrite the rules.

I ordered books on nonmonogamy. The most famous book in the category is *The Ethical Slut*, but I didn't buy that one. My reasoning: the title felt too glib. I didn't feel like a slut, not in a good way or a bad way. The word didn't fit, no matter how thoroughly it might have been reclaimed, liberated, reframed on its own terms. *Love in Abundance* had a similar linguistic problem: the title had the word *love* in it, and we were hoping to avoid that. I also passed on *When Someone You Love Is Polyamorous*, because when I Googled the phrase "when someone you love is," the first suggestion that popped up to complete it was "making bad choices."

The first book I bought was *Opening Up: A Guide to Creating and Sustaining Open Relationships*. This struck my ears as hopeful and appropriately sober. I also got *More Than Two: A Practical Guide to Ethical Polyamory*, though it sounded possibly too sober, like a grad school seminar. That would be good, though—a degree and diploma, a seal of approval, something sturdy to assure me that we could do this.

Opening our marriage, the books said, would require a tremendous amount of talking. We would have to commit to clear and often radically open communication. The fabric of any relationship needs tending and, over time, mending, and if we made our relationship nonmonogamous, it would require more attention, not less. The weave of our fabric would become more complex, requiring adroit management to avoid knots and fraying.

Say it all, I remember thinking. *Keep talking to each other. Just keep talking.* And—this one loomed large—*do not say anything you don't mean.* How often, in everyday conversation, had I said things I didn't mean or feel, just to be polite, to make things easier? How often had I said to Brandon what I thought I should say in order to maintain order, to repair a rift? We had never been good at disagreement. One of us always gave in when it got too uncomfortable. One of us would recognize that we were at a dead end, would begin to back out. We rarely paved a road through to the other side. We rarely stuck with it long enough to forge any kind of new, if painful, understanding.

If I wanted an open marriage, and if I wanted it to work, I had to get comfortable with uncomfortable conversations. Wanting this made me feel bold. I would rise to the occasion.

We spent two months talking about opening our marriage before we did anything about it. We went back to couples' counseling, this time with a new therapist experienced in working with nonmonogamous couples. It would be a process, and we wanted to get it right. There were moments when we felt together in it. There were moments when we screamed at each other. There are moments I am glad for. The more we talked, the more we learned, the closer we felt. It seemed inevitable, and right, that we should be taking this step. Nonmonogamy would be troublesome and difficult, but monogamy is troublesome and difficult too. To look at them side by side, to interrogate them both as valid ways of living—we'd never done this, never thought to.

I don't know if monogamy makes sense to me anymore, Brandon announced one day.

I nodded in agreement, swallowed hard, forced back a grin. I had brought us to this point, and I'd been terrified that he would regret it. To hear that he didn't—that he was even gaining from this tendentious contemplation—had to be a sign. We'd be okay.

What we were talking about was *us*. For the first time since our wedding, we put language to our commitment. We cheered: we got to decide what we were and what we weren't! This was *our* marriage, and we could write the rules however we wanted. We felt like pioneers on the frontier of our lives. The freedom we were after, we would build it ourselves! I alternated between euphoria and a searing anxiety, adrenaline pumping through me like I was being chased. This confused me, because I was also the one giving chase.

Here's what we decided: we'd remain each other's primary partner. In the language of open relationships, this meant that we'd give each other priority, the bulk of our time and energy. It meant that we were committed to a shared future with shared goals and a shared home. We also had a child together, and she would come above anything and anyone else. We agreed that June should not be impacted, especially not negatively, by the opening of our marriage. It had nothing to do with her.

Anyone else we dated would be a secondary partner. We would be open with each other about who we were seeing, and we would communicate with trust and clarity when it came to scheduling. We would have to be generous with each other, each making time for the other—and for the other to be with others. I wanted to date a woman, a queer or lesbian woman. I did not want Brandon to vet my partners, nor did I want to vet his. Brandon didn't feel strongly either way, or didn't say he did. Anyway, I had a husband and a child: What queer woman, what lesbian, would want to date me? And what straight woman would want to get with a married man? We commiserated, encouraged each other. We were both afraid of failing, and of succeeding.

The sticking point remained love. We couldn't seem to get around it.

What happens if you fall in love? Brandon asked. I don't want you to.

I don't want to either, I said.

But what happens if you do?

I felt my insides ball up, like I'd been scolded. I couldn't let myself consider the possibility of love: the thought was too painful, too pointed a reminder that I was steering us into murky waters. So I'd point the conversation in another direction instead: If we'd let ourselves interrogate monogamy, I'd ask, why not interrogate love? We'd allowed ourselves to question why sex with someone else should necessarily hurt our relationship, and *Pffft*, we'd answered, *how narrow-minded*. We were bigger than that. So why should love be a threat? Is there not enough to go around? If we—we as a couple—were capable of more than we'd previously imagined, why not this too?

I began to see myself as someone who could love more than one person at a time. Hadn't I said, anyway, that I wanted to know what it was like to be *loved* by a woman who loved women? *Loved*—that was the word that I'd reached for.

I, I, I. There was so much *I.* Even I could hear it. We never worried about him falling in love, only me. Of course we knew.

When Elio, the narrator of André Aciman's novel *Call Me by Your Name*, finds himself fantasizing about a man, a visiting grad student named Oliver, Elio longs for a night with him—a single night, even just an hour—to figure out if the attraction is real. "What I didn't realize," Elio explains, "was that wanting to test desire is nothing more than a ruse to get what we want without admitting that we want it."[18]

*

An old friend emailed in early April and wanted to catch up. Could I do a Saturday night? My friend was a lesbian, though we'd never talked much about it before. Now we had something new in common: I could tell her about jury duty, about the past several months, about our open marriage. Maybe she could fix me up. We decided to meet at Dino's, which had been open for a month—admittedly an odd choice given the situation, but this friend knew Brandon, and she wanted to see it. Brandon would be working there that night too. So I would meet up with my lesbian friend at my husband's restaurant, with my husband across the room, and she and I would hash out my desire to sleep with women.

I asked my mother to babysit, and she offered to have June sleep over. I put on jeans and a white sweat shirt, the neckline of which I'd trimmed *Flashdance*-style, so it tipped off one shoulder. I wore a bra with hot pink straps. At Dino's our friend hugged Brandon, and he gave her a tour. The bar was crowded, everything glowing neon red. I was sweating, that panicked sweat with its own peculiar smell. I had to get outside. I squeezed Brandon's shoulder, pulled him in for a hug, told him I'd be back in a couple of hours, and steered my friend out onto the sidewalk.

We ordered Negronis at a bar down the block. She told me about her recent breakup. I told her about Nora. I sat next to her and wondered if we looked like we were on a date. I hadn't imagined it that way, but could it be? Did she feel it too? Could it be this easy? I swiveled a little to face her, let my elbow bump into hers. Was there anyone I knew in this bar? Anyone who knew me, who knew Brandon, who knew me as June's mother? What would happen to us, all of us, if I kissed my friend?

I leaned toward her, and she laughed. Then her face was right there in front of me, and I went in, catching her top lip between my two. She was so soft, my head went blank, as though a curtain dropped. Even when Brandon was freshly shaved, he wasn't soft like this. She opened her mouth and took my bottom lip, sucked it between her teeth.

I should go, she said against my cheek. I've got an early meeting tomorrow.

Stay, I said. I want to kiss you.

She smiled. Aren't you worried someone will see? Come on, she said, rising from the stool. She was standing by my hip. I turned and clasped her elbow. She dropped to me and met my mouth square-on, so firm I felt the bones behind her skin. I searched her with my tongue.

You should reach out to Nora, she said, righting herself.

No, no—it was all in my head, I said. There wasn't anything there.

Well, you should find out for sure.

The next morning, Brandon, June, and I had plans with my mother to take the ferry to Bainbridge Island—a day-trip, just for fun, with Sunday lunch in a French restaurant and ice cream after. We drove my car. June had taken a spill the evening before, my mom reported. She fell face-first onto the asphalt outside the house, and her lip had gushed blood.

I cried for a long time, Mama, June said.

What I heard was: while I was out kissing a woman, my three-year-old fell on her face in the street.

On the ferry we climbed the stairs and found a bench by the window, and I pulled June onto my lap. There was a gash in the tender flesh of her lip, though not too bad. But something was wrong with her left front tooth: a fine gray line ran down it, gum to tip. During lunch I paced outside the restaurant, on hold with the dentist. She had X-rays taken the next morning: the tooth was cracked through to the root, would have to be pulled. June would be missing a front tooth for three or four years, until the adult tooth came in.

The day after the extraction, I took a picture of what we, with flinching cheer, called her "new smile." She's wearing a T-shirt with a lemon painted on the front, squint-grinning at the camera, her nose scrunched up like a cartoon mouse. She's fine. But what do I do with this? There was no direct line of causation between my child getting hurt and me. My absence did not gash her lip or crack her tooth. But I'd had a choice, hadn't I, and I'd been away from her. Brandon had been absent too, but he was just doing his job. June fell, and I was out kissing a woman in a bar.

Later that week I woke one morning with my head vibrating. What tethered it to my shoulders seemed less bone and muscle than live current. Maybe I had the stomach flu. I thought I could feel my intestines spin somehow, like thumbs twiddling. I should skip my morning coffee. I managed a little cereal, but it was hard to eat with my head this way. My insides felt heavy in comparison, though it was mostly empty in there. I had a dermatologist appointment in midmorning, an annual mole-and-freckle check, and I stopped afterward for a ginger ale. It was spicy going down, made me burp. I managed some toast for lunch. I thought about kissing my friend, and my gut turned over like a page.

That night I was supposed to be a guest speaker in a class at the university, an extension course taught by an acquaintance. Brandon was at Delancey, so I'd booked a babysitter. She came at five thirty, and I kissed June good night, since I'd miss bedtime.

On campus, I parked in the underground lot beneath the central plaza. The sky was still light as I stepped out of the elevator and made my way along a brick-paved path to the building where the class would meet. Sweat prickled my temples. I probably should have canceled, shouldn't be walking into a classroom with these germs. Maybe it wasn't contagious? Things had been stressful; maybe it was catching up with me. In the hallway outside the classroom I stopped to lean against the wall, its pimpled surface cool through my shirt. The nausea subsided, and I knocked on the door. I spoke to the students for an hour, and then I said something about needing to relieve the babysitter, hugged the friend who'd invited me, and left as fast as I'd come.

I was in the parking-garage elevator when I understood what was going to happen. There was no one around when I stepped out at my floor. In the concrete hallway I made it a few steps before doubling over. It was all ginger ale, a watery puddle on the concrete. I was wearing cheap black boots, faux suede, and it had splashed onto the toes. I stood and took an inventory: I was otherwise intact. I felt almost proud. *Look at me! A disaster, but upright!*

I took a few more steps down the hallway. I knew it was going to happen again. There was a trash can, but the lid was on it. Too late. I missed my shoes this time, silently commended myself. I hurried to the car before anyone could see what I'd done, unzipped my boots and tossed them in the trunk. My mouth tasted like bad milk. There was a napkin in the glove box, and I dragged it over my tongue, as though it would do anything.

At home, I fumbled in the dark on the side of the house, jammed the boots into the garbage bin. I knew I'd never get the smell out. I went inside in my socks. I must have offered some excuse to the babysitter.

I brushed my teeth and stood in the doorway to June's room. She had no idea what I'd been up to lately, what her father and I were doing. How could I ever want anything but to be here with her? The light from the hall touched her round cheek, pale as the moon.

Nausea woke me at midnight. Now I knew what to do. I bolted to the bathroom, lifted the toilet lid, and got on my knees. I could hear the tap running in the kitchen. Brandon was home. I was breathing hard. I pressed the length of my forearms into my thighs and leaned over the bowl, but nothing came up. In my lap, I noticed that my hands were closing. I tried to open my fingers, using one hand to tug at the other, but they were stuck. We'd taught American Sign Language to June as a baby: milk, water, please, flower, book, more. More, my hands said. I was panting. More air, need more air.

Are you okay? Brandon said. He was in the doorway. What's wrong, babe?

I puked tonight, I said, after my talk at the UW. I was whispering. My bathrobe was too hot. Somehow I was wearing my bathrobe. The tops of my feet hurt, mashed into the floor under my folded-over body.

Are you okay? he asked again. He stood behind me now, one foot on either side of my knees. There was his sock, gray at the toe. There were his hands in my hair. The space behind my eyes was too small. I decided to sit down, no more kneeling. I rocked onto one hip, braced against the wall of the bathtub with one of my clamped-up hands, which were now buzzing like they'd fallen asleep. My wrists were busy cramping now too, each contracting inward. I slid my feet out from under me, tried to wiggle my ankles, but look! there they went too, my ankles like my wrists, curling in, yanking each heel toward the other.

This must be a seizure. I'm having a seizure. Someone was gasping, a sucked-in half-sob.

I had to tell Brandon. He needed to see this, what was happening. What was happening?

June's room was across the hall, maybe five steps away. I imagined her standing in the doorway in her floral-print underwear from Target, eyes frosted with sleep, blinking into the bathroom. *Please don't let her wake up.* How could she not wake up? My head was too loud. I gave a croak. Brandon said something, and I worked to hear it.

I'm going to call the doctor, he said. And then, Can you hear me? Should I call your mom? And, Can you hear me?

There he was, down by my feet. There was no way they'd work

anymore, those feet. I turned the room on its side, started a slow descent to the terrycloth rug in front of the sink. A weird hardening spread outward from my mouth across my cheeks, like crystals of ice linking across the surface of water. Brandon was running out of the room. I rolled onto my back.

Here he was. He climbed over me, knelt, and poked something at my mouth.

Can you open? Open your mouth, he said. The doctor said to try to get you to drink something.

I thought about my lips, told them to open. The straw bumped against my teeth, and I pulled at it. Cold juice ran out, apple. It was one of June's juice boxes. I swallowed. The dog barked, and then my mother was in the doorframe. Brandon had called her too. She'd put on leggings and running shoes and a ponytail like always, like it wasn't midnight. I saw her seeing me. She held her voice steady and spoke to Brandon, to the air above me. What were they saying? The juice box belched, empty.

They told me it was only minutes, but it felt like hours that I was lying on the floor. My face was starting to thaw. They said it might have been the juice, the restoration of a reasonable blood sugar level. Or the act of drinking it, which required me to breathe. They decided I should go to the hospital and asked if I could stand up. I nodded. It was ten minutes to the emergency room. My mother drove, and we were silent, no radio. Why wasn't Brandon with me, and my mother back with June? My mother knew nothing. What catastrophe did she imagine for me?

The emergency room waiting area was empty. We were given our own room, and the nurse helped me onto a gurney. I still had my bathrobe on. My mother sat in a chair by my elbow and texted Brandon to say we'd arrived. As the nurse drew my blood, the TV on the wall threw off noiseless flashes of white-blue light.

Have you been under a lot of stress lately? the nurse asked.

Yeah, I whispered. I wanted to be a good patient. I wasn't going to lie. But I knew that whatever I said, my mother would hear. This would have to be it. I watched the ceiling.

Can you tell me what's been going on? the nurse asked.

I've been having kind of a weird time, I said. I figured out that I don't think I'm straight. My husband and I just opened up our marriage.

It seems you've had a panic attack, the nurse said. She patted me on the shoulder. Let's get you some rest. Then she handed me an Ativan and a paper cup of water. This was how I came out to my mother.

It was a notable omission, not saying anything earlier to her. I never feared being ostracized, preached at, beaten up, packed off to conversion therapy, or any of the tragic and even deadly consequences that coming out can lead to. I had the luxury of knowing that I would be okay. But my mother is my only living parent, and I didn't want to upset her, disappoint her.

I had told her nothing because I had hoped it would blow over. Given enough time, enough muscle, there wouldn't be anything to come out about. Why talk about a hypothetical? And it wasn't like I was single, able to accommodate my desire without repercussions for others; I was married, I was a mother.

Coming out would not only be about my sexuality—which, for all its peril, at least has nice cultural precedents. My mother is a Rachel

Maddow fan. Six months after jury duty, my mother invited me out to see *Carol*. She loves going to the movies; this was just another film for her. Sitting in the theater, I said nothing about its peculiar resonance. To come out, I'd have to also come out about our open relationship. However I explained it, I knew it would look like a blazing red flag to most people. I knew this because it looked like a red flag to me. I reminded myself that plenty of healthy marriages are open, even if the noisy and dominant norm is monogamy. I repeated this to myself with the shaky fervor of a new convert: *Our marriage is valid, no matter its parameters.* It was valid before, and it was valid now. I did not want to be divorced, a divorcée. I did not want June to be a child of divorce, shuttling back and forth between houses, towing her purple *Frozen* suitcase with "Family Forever" in curling script across the lid. Divorce would be a failure, a public admission of error, a giant fucking mess.

No, I didn't want to talk about it. What Brandon and I were doing, it belonged to the province of *us*. We owed no explanation. We were a team, us versus the world. And isn't that marriage: to be united against the world's demands, sorrows, and pain? To keep it between us, as something that *we* were working on, would be a testament to our bond, to *us* as a unit.

I had said nothing because I knew my mother would be afraid for us. I knew what her fear would look like, the firm set of her jaw as she took it all in. I was afraid of her silence because the contents of my head would rush in to fill it. I could have filled swimming pools, municipal reservoirs, with shame. She'd think I was crazy. My mother would have some kind of judgment, even if she never said a word. In the emergency room that night, she said little: *I'm glad you're okay.* She didn't have to say more for me to hear it. I feared her judgment because it was my own.

11

I thought I knew myself, I said. Until Nora, I really thought I did. What the hell happened to me?

My therapist uncrossed his legs, recrossed them in the other direction.

What if you think of it this way, he said. Imagine you went to a doctor, and they told you that you had cancer. They started to plot out a course of treatment, but you said, "No! Stop! I won't start treatment until I know *how*, and *why*, I got this." Do you really need answers before you can start to heal?

But but but, I said.

Another approach.

Let's say you're a writer, I said. Say something strange has happened to you, and you want to write a story about it. The story has got to make sense somehow. If it doesn't make sense, it doesn't work.

Go on, my therapist said.

When I was thirty-six years old, I became fixated on a woman I hardly knew. I'd felt pretty straight for my whole life, straight enough to call myself "straight." Now I was obsessed with a woman. That sounds crazy, doesn't it?

I'm listening, he said.

Here I thought I knew myself. I must have missed something. I can't be crazy. This is the only explanation: I just missed the signs.

So I do this whole archeological dig on myself, comb through every story of every person I've ever wanted or dated or loved, looking for glimmers of gayness. I want to find that it was in me all along, because I'd rather be clueless than crazy. See, I've got to make sense! People *cohere*. If they don't, they must be nuts, and I'm not nuts. I'm just clueless, that's all.

Sure, the therapist says. I've heard that story. It's true for a lot of people. But if you're hoping to find evidence that confirms the story you want to tell, you're going to find it. Not because it's actually there but because you're biased. It's confirmation bias: you'll find it because you *want* to find it.

I looked past him out the window, wondering how long I could stare at the sunlight bouncing off the windshield of a car parked across the street.

Your whole life has been true. It happened to you. All that time that you felt straight, when you dated men, when you married Brandon—all of what you felt was real. But this story you're trying to tell, it's not your story. I think you want your story to be a straight line, but it may not be.

Then what *is* my story? Tell me.

So what if you don't "cohere," or not all the time? Imagine the perspective of someone who meets you at a party. They see you dancing. It seems like you're outgoing and fun. But a different person, let's say someone who meets you at a coffee shop, might describe you as reserved or shy. You're focused on your work; you don't make eye contact. Both people can be right. Sometimes you're this; sometimes you're that.

But that's just mood, I said. That's not my *self*.

I know you want to think there's a firm thing that's "Molly." Some core that you can understand and count on. But if there is a core to you, what exactly is it? This is more uncomfortable to think about. What part of you is stable, if you're actually changing all the time? You didn't used to be a mother, or a wife, or a restaurant owner. Now you are. That's a lot of change. What if the one constant thing about you is that you're changeable?

Problem: Even I do not believe that my experience is possible. Unless. *Theory A*: I was born gay, or bi, but I did not understand it until now. *Or, Theory B*: I changed, almost beyond my own recognition.

Theory A fits the common understanding of sexual orientation. I saw a glimpse when I was twenty, with Laura, but I have been closeted for most of my life. I have deceived even myself. I clothed myself in layers of self-deception. (How on earth did I do it?) Even while telling myself that I loved Brandon to the exclusion of all others, loved him enough to marry him, somewhere deep within me lived this person who would give anything to fuck a woman. She'd stowed away inside my psyche for *years*, hiding belowdecks without making a sound.

Theory B is of course simpler. I changed.

I read in Maggie Nelson's *The Red Parts* that Nelson's mother once sent her a card to celebrate a poetry publication, and on the card was that famous Joan Didion line: "We tell ourselves stories in order to live." Nelson was unsettled by it.

"I became a poet in part because I didn't want to tell stories," she writes. "As far as I could tell, stories may enable us to live, but they also trap us, bring us spectacular pain. In their scramble to make sense of nonsensical things, they distort, codify, blame, aggrandize, restrict, omit, betray, mythologize, you name it. This has always struck me as cause for lament, not celebration."[19]

It looks like I'm having a midlife crisis, I thought. *That's what this is.*

But it didn't feel like I'd imagined a midlife crisis would feel. Yes, I'd asked for an open marriage. I'd had a panic attack on the bathroom floor. But under the panic, I knew why I did what I was doing: because I couldn't not do it. I had changed.

Nora met me like an enzyme, and she catalyzed a reaction. And I couldn't undo it, because *it* was not other from me. It *was* me.

12

Hi, Nora, I wrote. I found your email address online, and I hope it's okay to contact you. I was a juror on the trial last summer, and you mentioned that you were a writer. What are you working on these days? Would you be up for coffee sometime?

I sent the email before I could decide not to. I held my breath. The time stamp read 9:28 P.M., April 20, 2016. I imagined her struggling to place my name, to even remember our having met ten months ago.

Her reply came at 9:49: Hi, I was recently thinking I wanted to catch up with you!

She'd been thinking of me. Exclamation point!

I don't remember the days between sending the email and seeing Nora again. We agreed to meet that Sunday afternoon at a coffee shop across town. I got there first. Nerves chattered my teeth. I ordered a beer, found a table facing the window, and took out my laptop as though I planned to work. Out on the sidewalk I saw her reaching for the door handle. I stared at the laptop screen. She was wearing jeans, a button-down shirt, and a thin sweater in dark green. I'd never seen her out of a suit. From the corner of my eye, I watched her walk to another table, stop to greet and hug someone there, then notice me. I forced my eyes up. She smiled, striding toward my table. Her smile was exactly as I remembered it: quick, wide, white as whole milk. I stood to hug her, as though it were easy.

We talked about the trial. It felt natural, or we both worked hard to create the illusion that it was. I asked about her work, her writing. She asked about my work, and I told her about the restaurants, about Brandon and June. I said lots of things to avoid saying anything, or everything. Then she said it: Are you queer?

I must have been plain as a sheet of glass. How long had she been thinking of asking this? I thought I'd hidden myself so well.

I fumbled. I talked obliquely about a recent crush on a woman, said my husband and I had opened our marriage, were trying it out. Words came from my mouth like they were someone else's.

I've dated people in open relationships, she said.

A thought: *If this were fiction, a good editor would scratch this scene out.*

She continued. I've had a crush on you since the trial, she said. I'd love to date you.

We went out the next Saturday, the last day of April. I parked on the street outside the city park where we'd agreed to meet. Nora waited for me on a bench by the reflecting pool. She had a fresh haircut. It was tidy around her ears, trimmed close along the back of her head. I thought about dragging my fingers up, nape to crown, against the prickle of her hair. I could do that now, if I wanted to. She wanted me to touch her, didn't she? She was here.

She sat at one end of the bench, and I sat down at the other. We were too far apart, weirdly far apart. Nausea swam around my gut like a strange fish.

I brought something for you, she said. It's my favorite book about writing. Do you have it?

She handed me a package wrapped in twine. It was a paperback copy of *On Writing Well*, by William Zinsser. I didn't have it. On the title page, she'd written the date and an inscription. Her handwriting was even and relaxed, the *M* of my name a cheerful zigzag, the *o* flowing into looping *l*s, a neat up-and-down *y*.

She had written my name! I goggled at it, like a preteen running into her school crush in the toothpaste aisle at Target: *Whoa, he brushes his teeth, just like me.* Nora had written my name. This is what it looks like when her hand forms my name! I couldn't look directly at her, or the web of muscle at the corner of my eye would seize.

For a while we talked about the weather, which was unseasonably warm. Nora had rolled her jeans once at the hem, where they rested on the creased cowboy boots she'd worn in court. I stared at a hedge in front of me, noticed that its leaves were the size and shape of almonds. We set off for a bar. Walking beside her, I saw that she wasn't as tall as I'd thought. I realized I'd never done this before: I'd never walked beside her. It felt different from walking beside anyone else. I was walking beside Nora. I was walking beside a woman who was gay, and who looked gay, and I was not walking beside this woman because she was my friend. I was walking beside her because we wanted to put our tongues in each other's mouths.

I took her to a bar owned by a friend. I wanted to make it all seem ordinary. I needed this to be ordinary. I'd texted the friend ahead of time with a forcefully matter-of-fact heads-up, told her I'd figured out that I wasn't straight, *la la la,* that Brandon and I had opened our relationship, that if she saw me at the bar, looking datey with a woman, that was why. Our friend must have told the bartender, who was an acquaintance. When he saw me with Nora, he smiled and introduced himself to her, and then he bought us a round. He unfurled a semblance of normalcy over us, light as a blanket on sand.

We ate tacos on the same side of the banquette. I put my feet up on a chair, and so did she. By unspoken agreement, we did not allow them to touch. We could have gone up in flames.

Are you sure your husband is okay with this? she said. How does he feel about it?

I reassured her. I said he'd gone out one night this week and had let himself flirt a bit. I didn't want to talk about him.

The street was empty as we walked to my car. We stopped on the sidewalk beside a brick house with expensively pruned hedges. Something wobbled in my stomach, went zinging up between my ears. Can I kiss you? I asked, and then I did.

Her mouth was open just enough. My lips found her upper lip just right of center, and I kissed the ridge where it met the skin above. Her tongue moved gently, a polite suggestion. I felt her mouth close around my lower lip, and I drove myself against her, linked my hands at the small of her back. Her breasts pressed against my chest. They were bigger than mine, pliant the way a waterbed is, and they made a peculiar spacer between us. I'd never collided this way with familiar and foreign, like-me and not-me. I'd never been this close to another woman, not since I was an infant with my mother. Nora and I were not the same person, but she knew what it felt like to have breasts, to have a vagina, to live in a body like this, to move it through the world, to move it against another body. This was a new intimacy: the pleasure of sameness. Her thigh slid between my legs and offered itself to me. I pressed my pelvis against the firm pad of her muscle and gave her my own thigh in return. We fit, because she was made like me. She whispered into my mouth and I pulled in her words like air.

I still have my calendar from 2016. In the square for that Saturday, the day of my first date with Nora, I wrote only a reminder to follow up on a freelance check I was waiting for and, at the bottom, the word *Nora*. Where was June while I was out? I have no record of it.

For our second date, Nora suggested a karaoke bar with private rooms. This was bold, and I liked it. Walking from my car, I caught her silhouette against a streetlamp at the end of the block, her hands shoved in the hip pockets of her jeans. She looked like a man, like a woman who looks like a man. She held her back straight, her stance wide. Her shoulders were square above the sloping dunes of her chest. I liked the contradictions of her body. A thought came like an elbow to the ribs, or a wink: *She's waiting for you, kid.* I wanted to run to her.

She'd reserved a room for us, closet-size and dim, at the end of a corridor. We sat down on a leather bench along one wall, close enough that our legs touched. I couldn't believe I was with her. Would I ever get used to this? Did I want to? I slid my arm along the bench behind her, and we pulled at our beers and queued up songs before we could chicken out: "9 to 5," "Edge of Seventeen," and "You Belong with Me"—a duet, so on-the-nose it smarted. I couldn't look at her when we sang. When would we kiss? The knowledge that we would, of course we would, rose steadily along my spine like an airplane gaining altitude. I climbed onto her lap and took her face in my hands. When I touched her, her skin was smooth, a woman's.

Can we go to your house? I said.

I don't know, she said shyly.

Why not? I bit her lip. I thought she was teasing.

I don't think we should sleep together yet, she said.

I ran my hand over her hair, as spiny as cut grass, and bit her again.

No, really, she said. I don't want to be the first pancake. You know how people always throw out the first pancake?

I laughed. I never do that! I said. I love the first pancake. Then I leaned in closer and said: I wouldn't do that to you.

She led the way to her house. There was a sectional in the front room, and we climbed onto it. I felt beneath her shoulder blades for the band of her bra. It was a sports bra, racer-back, tight as a bandage. She smelled like Dove soap and, up close, Old Spice deodorant. I wanted her skin on my skin. I peeled off my shirt, tugged at the hem of hers. She took my hand and squeezed it, then pressed it away.

Not yet, she said.

Hadn't we both dreamed of this moment for months? Why would she want to stop? But to question her seemed pushy, insensitive. She was right to take it slow. We should be careful not to hurt each other.

We stretched out on our sides, and she wriggled her hand into the back pocket of my jeans. We stared at each other, grinning.

You don't have your ears pierced, she said. She had two empty holes in each ear.

No, I never wanted it, I said. It never felt like me.

That's amazing, she said, that you've always known yourself so well. She squeezed my ass.

I smiled, pleased, and didn't correct her.

So you're dating a woman, a friend said to me over lunch. Can I ask you something? I don't know how to phrase this, but I think it's interesting that you're dating a woman who looks so—masculine.

You can phrase it like that, I said. I think I like the juxtaposition of it, you know? The presence of both.

I was learning what I wanted, and I applied myself to it like a student. Nora and I had the same chromosomes and the same parts. But we had different relationships to our gender. She queered the notion of *woman*, keeping her hair in a conservative businessman's cut and standing with her legs set wide as a bouncer. She wore suits to court and, to see me, tucked-in oxfords with a modest two buttons undone. She had breasts, but she kept them pressed tight to her chest. She walked the line between man and woman, smudged it under her foot.

I'd grown up watching "It's Pat" on *Saturday Night Live*, a series of sketches about an androgynous, socially awkward character played by Julia Sweeney. *SNL*'s "Pat" sketches were a runaway success; they recurred from 1990 to 1994 and were even made into a movie. Pat was thick and short, with a lumpy torso under a blue Western shirt and tan belted pants. Pat was oblivious to the confused tittering that erupted when they walked into a room. The other characters in the sketch were always trying (and failing) to determine Pat's gender, and if Pat mentioned dating, others reacted with revulsion. We kids thought this was hilarious, and we liked to do Pat imitations at recess. Androgyny: none of us knew the word, but we understood it as a pitiable mistake, a glitch in the system. We understood that there was a real thing—a *real* woman, a *real* man—that Pat was failing to be.

What I had understood of *woman* stood in contrast to what I understood of *man*. They gestured at each other across a divide, defined themselves in contrast, made themselves solid. There were two natural and essential sexes: a woman and a man. Binary sexes appear so real, so normal, as to seem inevitable. I remember reading Judith Butler in graduate school and sort of getting it, but also not getting it at all: "Gender appears to the popular imagination as a substantial core . . . the spiritual or psychological correlate of biological sex," she wrote. "Performing one's gender wrong"—like *SNL*'s Pat—"initiates a set of punishments both obvious and indirect, and performing it well provides the reassurance that there is an essentialism of gender identity after all."[20]

I had scoffed at the scripts of womanhood that my childhood in Oklahoma City had offered me, but I'd believed all the same that there were right ways to do it, right and wrong ways to be a woman. My mother was a right way. I had always wanted to be good. I had stood by my husband, even as he made choices that I didn't want. I'd raged, but I had recommitted again and again. I'd panted to do it all right. *Can I be someone who can live with this?* I'd contorted like an acrobat.

When I saw Nora in the courtroom, I knew only that she was a woman in a suit. But I think she looked like something more than that, something I didn't have: the will to stand apart, to crumple up the script. She seemed to define herself against no one, yet she was as real as anyone else. She was both and neither, somewhere in between, someone else entirely. She was her own invention, and I wanted her.

There was no mistake or glitch about Nora. The friction between her body and the strictures of the world—that friction didn't read as failure. Instead, it gave off heat.

We had sex for the first time in her bed, early one afternoon. We'd been dating for three weeks. I drove to her house with Beyoncé's *Lemonade* on the stereo, turned up until the dash vibrated. I knew what we were going to do.

I was nervous when I walked in the door. I didn't want to be shy with her, but I couldn't shake it. She must have felt it, too. We lumbered through a greeting, small-talked.

It was daylight, and her sheets were patterned in beige and white. *There are no men here*, I remember thinking. We could be anything. When she lifted her T-shirt over her head, there were three freckles along the ridge of her collarbone, dark as ink and evenly spaced. Orion's Belt. We would find our way.

I'd set an alarm on my phone so I wouldn't be late to pick up June, after. I wondered if anyone at school would notice that I was different. *Was* I different? Was I the same person I'd been all along, before that afternoon, before that spring, before jury duty?

June and I stopped for eggs at the grocery store. She wanted cherries too, and I let her pick out a bag of them. At home we made dinner, put unicorn Band-Aids on each other for fun, waited for Brandon. He didn't have to work that night, so he'd be home to eat with us. What did I tell him about Nora? He knew where I'd been that afternoon, but

I don't remember the conversation. What I remember is how proud I was of us, him and me, for pulling it off.

June helped set the table, as she was learning how to do. Brandon made a salad. I warmed beans and boiled seven-minute eggs, rinsed the cherries and piled them in a bowl. We sat together around our table with its stack of bills at one end and mail-in ballots for the 2016 primaries. June spat cherry pits onto her plate, gleeful, her face and hands splotched with hot-pink juice.

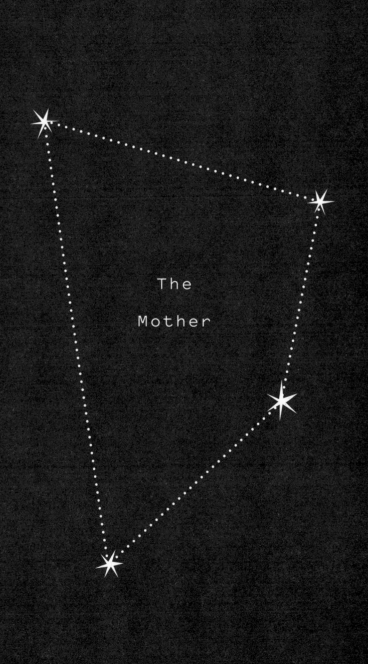

The

Mother

13

I have a photo of us, June and me, taken that week. We're at the dining counter in Delancey, and June sits on my lap in a blue dress, her body perpendicular to mine. I think Brandon took the picture: he would have been working the pizza oven that night. I've got a fork in one hand and a plate of asparagus in front of me, and my other arm wraps around June's narrow back. It must be close to bedtime. Her eyes are a little glazed, focused somewhere below the camera, and she sucks her thumb, holding a hank of her hair in the same hand. She's done that since she was an infant. You can't see my face because I'm looking down, and my bangs have fallen in the way, my chin tucked against her forehead. You can see that I am her mother.

She would be four soon. For nearly four years I had fed her and clothed her and read to her and bathed her and told her I loved her, and at bedtime I always sang "Twinkle, Twinkle" twice, the house rule. It took juggling to date Nora while being a mother and a wife. Was I doing it well enough? Was I a bad mother? My skull buzzed like a radio between stations. I find it difficult now to recall the individual days of that spring; their residue is mostly a feeling. I was happy.

What does one "owe" to one's children? What does it mean to have their best interests in mind? What does that look like? When I put my mouth on Nora's mouth, I did not look like someone who had her child's best interests in mind. I was not a parent in that particular moment. But when I put my mouth on Nora's mouth, I felt like *me*, a fully fleshed me. When I went home to June, that's the mother I brought to her.

What is a mother? To a newborn baby, its primary caregiver—usually its mother—is everything. She is food, shelter, life. A mother is so fully adapted to her infant's needs, explains British pediatrician and psychoanalyst D. W. Winnicott, that the child imagines its mother's breast to be a part of itself. This is an illusion, of course, and it can't last. It also *should not* last, according to Winnicott. A child's sense of self depends not upon it having a perfect mother but a "good-enough mother."[21] Winnicott's good-enough mother is one who slowly retreats, who adapts less and less completely to her infant as the child matures and becomes able to handle frustration and disappointment. Our mothers' failure to meet our every need teaches us a crucial lesson: that our mother is a separate, finite entity, and that there's a difference between *me* and *not-me*. From her "failure," Winnicott argues, we form our first sense of self.

Winnicott articulated this idea more than half a century ago, but we're still wrestling with the image of the perfect mother—as though she existed, as though she *should* exist. I want to be a perfect mother to June, though my sense of what that means changes almost constantly, as my child changes. If not a perfect mother, I want at least to be good. I want more than to do no harm; I want to know that I have been a good mother by some codified, seal-of-approval standard, even though I know that the good mother June needs almost certainly looks different from someone else's. I want to be a good mother, though probably not even my child and I could agree on what that means.

I keep coming back to one thing: June belongs to me, in the sense that her body came from my body, in the sense that her care is my responsibility. But I do not own her. She's always been herself, only June, from her first cries and grunts. My work is to love her, guide her, and support her—no more and no less—as she becomes ever more real, more *June*. In this sense, I too belong to her. But she does not own me. I too am real. Surely I cannot be her mother if I am not also myself.

*

The last day of May, Nora sends me a text. She's in my part of town; how about she stops by? It's such a nice day. I close the laptop. Brandon's at the restaurant. Nora is on the stoop with a spray of tea roses. We drop onto the sofa and make out for a while. We've been dating for five weeks. Lying beneath her, I rub the collar of her white button-down between my thumb and index finger. I tell her I'm falling in love with her. She smiles, bashful. I can tell she isn't ready to say it, but I know well enough how she feels. Over on the table my phone rings, and I let it. A few minutes later, it rings again. Maybe ten minutes and then it rings again, a third time. I should get it. Nora sits up, and I roll off the couch. The caller's name is lit up: it's the school. It's 3:47. I was supposed to pick up June at three.

I've been in a meeting, I stammer, choking back a sob. Oh god, I'm so sorry! I lost track of time.

June is fine, says her teacher. No worries! She's in the aftercare room. Come when you can.

June is fine, but I am not. I'm so far from fine that I'll lie to Brandon about it that night, tell him I was reading on the sofa and fell asleep, didn't wake up until the phone rang.

Before I spent a night at Nora's, Brandon and I set parameters: what time I'd go, when I'd be back, what to tell June. I'd been away from her for work trips and a couple of family things, so we decided to keep it simple, tell her this was like that. I'd be back first thing in the morning. We consoled her with a special treat, something my parents had let me do when I was a kid and one of them was traveling: June could have a "slumber party" with Brandon in our bed.

It was disorienting at Nora's, sleeping in my city but in someone else's bed. Sleep was halting. It couldn't possibly be okay to be here. I was sure I'd be in trouble somehow. I wanted to be in Nora's bed, wanted to be drunk on her, wanted to feel the way I had in the coffee shop, when she told me she'd had a crush on me too and I almost passed out at the sound of it. Instead I lay in her bed, across town from our bed, where June sleepwalked her small, meaty, sweet-smelling feet across Brandon's back, and I felt like I was cleaving in two.

Brandon and I had committed ourselves to empathy and clear communication. But our efforts at talking often devolved into yelling. The arrangement was still new, but these didn't feel like growing pains. It felt like we were falling apart.

Brandon had been on some dates. He'd kissed someone. I knew he loved me and I loved him, and I wanted him to have a good time. But he was more conflicted, caught up in how odd it felt to be with someone else. We'd told a handful of friends about our open relationship, but we both fretted about being seen. The restaurant industry is small and close-knit: Where could we go in this town without running into someone? I wished I felt proud, maybe even indignant—this is normal, what's the fuss, etc.—but mostly I felt sheepish.

Taking a stab at transparency, we told the manager at Delancey what we were up to, in case she heard whispers. A couple of weeks later, having fielded a torrent of gossip, she advised us to tell the entire staff. In a surreal scene, we assembled our employees in the Delancey dining room and, after outlining a new policy on paid leave, I formally announced our open marriage.

We'd tried to convince ourselves that our marriage was strong enough, loving enough, flexible enough to accommodate the stretch we asked of it. Something about me had changed, but people are always changing, aren't they? Just look at Brandon: when we met, he was going to be a music professor, and now he was a chef with three restaurants. We'd changed. So what? What we were doing was natural, no more ill-considered than monogamy. But it almost never felt that way. Most days I wanted to puke. I watched Brandon try not to worry as I set off to see Nora. We were terrified. He could admit it before I could, because I was busy falling in love.

I remember sitting next to him on the sofa in our living room, the sofa where I'd made out with Nora. He'd come home for lunch, and we had a date to talk. Outside the window the sky was clear and unflinching, the color of a blue raspberry popsicle.

I think I'm falling in love with her, I said. The refrigerator motor gurgled. I didn't mean to, I added. I know that doesn't help, but it's true.

He was silent. A couch spring squeaked. I wanted to see what his face looked like, but I was afraid to turn my head.

It doesn't have to change anything, I said, not sure if I believed it. *We'd always been ourselves, hadn't we?* We'd been like this for a long time. We were discrete bodies, separate stars, but from the right vantage point, we'd aligned. We were a shape that made sense. We'd made a home for ourselves next to each other. But we'd never stood still, not really. We were always gliding, gradually, steadily, on our own trajectories.

"It is curious to me that people take straight lines for granted," writes Anne Truitt. "We never see them unless we make them ourselves; even the apparently straight horizon of the ocean against the sky curves if we see it from the air."[22]

Truitt had been contemplating Orion's Belt, three stars that appear, from our planet, to form a straight line. The configuration we call Orion is arbitrary, an artifact of our observation, as man-made as myth. When we speak its name, we point to a story. The ancient Greeks say he was one of Poseidon's sons, a great hunter, placed in the celestial sphere opposite the scorpion that killed him. In the winter Orion stalks the sky, massive and bright. When Scorpius rises in summer, he flees.

Outside of our minds, the stars we assign to a constellation bear no particular relationship to each other. Each star has the potential to be connect-the-dotted to any number of other stars. We may not see those shapes from here, but they are no less real.

I had lived in our constellation for some time, within the shape of the family we made. Three stars connected like fact: me, Brandon, our child. I navigated by the light of our hunter. Now I couldn't say what was more important: Orion's steadfast presence in our sky, or to speak the shape for what it is—a formation we made from our own stories, both true and subject to revision.

14

When my father died, a family friend gave me a copy of Donald Hall's *Without*, a collection of poems written after the death of his wife of twenty-three years, the poet Jane Kenyon. "Letter in Autumn" flattened me: the image of Hall cleaning out Kenyon's car to sell it, making an inventory of his grief in the form of her hair ties, cassette tapes, and a tin of saved fortune-cookie fortunes. I wanted to know more about old love. I wanted to know how people become lodestars to one another. I wanted to feel the slow burn of it.

The summer of Nora, I read somewhere about *Our World*, a book of photographs by the late Molly Malone Cook, with prose and poems by Cook's longtime partner, the poet Mary Oliver. I ordered it online and read it in one go, and when I looked up, I was crying. In all the years that Oliver and Cook were a couple, they were rarely apart, not even when Oliver traveled to teach. Cook would come along, and they'd make a home wherever they were.

"We were talkers—about our work, our pasts, our friends, our ideas ordinary and far-fetched," writes Oliver. "We would often wake before there was light in the sky and make coffee and let our minds rattle our tongues. . . . It was a forty-year conversation."[23]

My own longtime partnership looked nothing like this. Brandon and I were frequently apart, and the hours we were together were mostly spent sleeping. On the face of it, I knew this wasn't unusual: it's the experience of many couples who work full-time. But Brandon and I rarely woke at the same hour, and I was often asleep when he got home. Because of the restaurant schedule, we'd never had it any different, not since our earliest weeks of marriage. I'd had wild newlywed fantasies of nights at home, watching *Jeopardy!*, but that wasn't us. We didn't sit still much. We didn't get into bed early and read. We rarely talked beyond the businesses, and later, beyond June. It mostly worked, in that neither of us was suffering. I thought I was fine. I thought, *Well, these are the realities of adulthood*, and I wasn't wrong.

That summer I started to keep a journal. I want a simpler life, I wrote. I want to wake up with someone and drink coffee together. I want to take June to school and come home to my desk. I want to write again. I want to cook and eat a meal every night with the person I love. I want to lie around and read the Sunday *Times*. I want to climb the ladder to the roof and watch the sun go down. I want to live as a family.

For weeks, all we do is argue. In this new iteration of our marriage, an inverse proportion has been established: the happier I am, the worse off he is.

He can't get over my falling in love. At first, I am contrite: I know I did exactly what neither of us wanted me to do. He is allowed to dislike this situation, even to refuse to live with it. I've scared us both.

But as I struggle to reassure him, I am also thinking this: that my falling in love with another person has no real bearing, not forcibly, on our marriage. Remember, I say, we can write the rules here! It's complicated, I know, but my love is not a fixed quantity. I have enough to go around. Please believe me.

15

I liked my body with Nora's body. I had liked my body with a man's body too. But a flinty confidence radiated from the fact of her being a woman: *I know what it's like to have these parts*, her body said, *and how it feels.*

"When I am with her," writes Minnie Bruce Pratt, "I have no idea what sex I am or what gender, whose body I have or the meaning of my gestures."[24] I looked at my body as though I'd never seen it before. When Nora told me I was beautiful, I took it in and kept it close, like a picture in a locket. Had I not believed this when others had said it? The syntax seemed different. It made more sense.

The first time we'd had sex I circled the date in my calendar, then starred it for emphasis. Has anyone ever been so eager? I had a new range of motion, and I wanted every inch of it. Nora wore cotton boxer briefs, and I eased my fingers into the waistband. She batted my arm away, giggling. That tickles! she said. I wanted to make her feel good, but I would have to be taught.

Help me learn, I said. I kissed the ledge of her collarbone, slid my lips toward the arc of her breast. I wanted to get my whole body around her, like an amoeba.

Well, she said, I don't like to be penetrated. I don't like the feeling of it.

That's okay, I said. There's so much else we can do.

She took my hand and put it on the outside of her briefs. Here, she said, guiding my hand under her own. Press here, like this.

Through the thin cotton I could feel the contours of her, the place where one fold slipped against another. Her eyes closed, and I heard her breath hitch in her throat, like a door latching. Then her hand closed hard around my fingers, and she opened her eyes.

I'd rather make you come instead, she said, rolling to face me. She gave a small grin and shrugged. Can I put my mouth on you?

I nodded. Had I done something wrong? *Why won't she let me touch her?* The air above us felt thick, pressurized. I couldn't speak.

This was how it went for a while: she let me touch her for only a moment, on the outside of her briefs. She said she couldn't explain it; she just wanted to touch me instead. And she was good at it. I wanted her to touch me.

But I also wanted to touch her. I had never touched anyone's vulva, anyone's vagina, but my own. I wanted Nora so much, but I was also nervous: What would she feel like? Would she like it? Would *I* like it? What would she smell like, taste like? I wanted to touch her skin, not the fabric covering it.

I wanted to earn her trust. I loved the way she fucked me, loved the firm efficiency of her fingers, loved to look at her long eyelashes as she moved her mouth between my legs. I wanted to fuck her like that. I wanted to earn her trust. When the definition of sex is not a set thing, how do you hash it out? You talk. You talk before anything else. We talked and we talked.

One night she said I could touch her. I worked my hand slowly down the silk of her belly until I found the place where she was wet. A quiet flare of recognition behind my eyes: the body under my fingers felt like my own. This didn't happen with a man, with a man's body, because it couldn't. She was a heat I wanted to be inside, a hot bath. Her pelvis rose under my hand, pressure meeting pressure. Her thighs shook as she came. In the dark I beamed, phosphorescent with her pleasure.

I never entered her, and I never tried. She was naked with me only once, the first time we had sex. On that occasion I'd cupped my hand around her breast, felt her flinch.

Do you like this? I asked. Should I not?

No, no—it's fine.

No, but do you like having your breasts touched? I want to know what you like.

Yeah, she said. I do.

But there was something here. Did she not feel safe? Had I done something, had something happened to her? Was there something about her body—her breasts, her vagina, the womanly costume of her skin? I tried to ask.

Queer sex isn't like straight sex, she said. You can't just rip each other's clothes off.

Y-You can't? I stammered.

Could this be right? I know some queer people, I thought. *I've read books, watched shows, seen movies. I'm pretty sure queer people* do *rip each other's clothes off sometimes. Why make some broad claim about queerness? That can't be true, can it?* Irritation prickled at the back of my throat. *If she needs sex to be a certain way, why doesn't she just say it?*

Or maybe she is *saying it. Yes. She* is *saying what she wants. She is telling me about herself to the best of her ability.*

I felt the irritation give way to shame, hard as a lozenge. I didn't know how to be queer. I didn't know anything.

What do you mean exactly, I asked, about not ripping each other's clothes off? I don't understand. Are you talking about consent?

Queer sex just doesn't work this way, she said.

I wanted our sex to be a conversation, but we talked more than we fucked.

Kind of gross, even dangerous, isn't it, to bitch about a woman who won't have sex with you?

I felt gross for wanting anything. Nora could do, or not do, whatever she pleased with her body. She was a person, not my fantasy. Surely she'd be happier with a person who knew the rules. But I wanted to be her person, and she seemed to want me to be. I wasn't good, but she could make me good. I should hurry to catch up, to get it right.

I'd pried myself out of a frame that didn't fit, and now Nora and I would fit me for a new one. We worked to make the facts of me—a mother, a wife, someone who had lived her whole life in the straight world—square up alongside her. Could I be polyamorous? Could I be someone's lover? Could I be queer? Who would decide? I wanted to put my ear to her body like a shell, let her echo tell me who I was.

Can I go down on you? I asked. It had taken weeks to work up the guts.

She seemed to consider.

I'm usually a top, she said. Not a stone top, not entirely. But a top.

What do you mean by "stone top"? I said.

I mean, I don't really want to be touched. I don't need it. I'd rather touch you. I'd rather give than receive.

Is this queer sex? If she's a top, do I have to be a bottom? What if I want to be both? What if I want to be neither?

I said, I just want to be a person in bed with you.

16

One afternoon, June came home pouting. When I asked what was wrong, she said a girl in her class had called her a baby.

I murmured sympathies. I wanted to drive back to school and pummel the kid.

What do you think? I asked her. Do *you* think you're a baby?

June shook her head, dragged the back of her hand across her dripping nose. She was not quite four years old.

Then there you go, I said. You're not a baby, Junie. You know who you are.

Easier to say it to her than to say it to myself.

"Birth is not merely that which divides women from men," writes author Rachel Cusk. "It also divides women from themselves. . . . Another person has existed in her, and after their birth they live within the jurisdiction of her consciousness. When she is with them she is not herself; when she is without them she is not herself."[25]

September 7, 2012: I went into labor late on a Friday night. Each time a contraction came, I wrapped my arms around Brandon's neck and clung to him, hung from his chest in a perverse and painful slow dance. At five the next evening, sixteen hours into labor, I asked for an epidural. Another twelve hours later—twenty-eight hours into labor—I was ten centimeters dilated. As the sun rose that Sunday morning, I started to push.

Thirty minutes, an hour, an hour and a half. I started to panic: I was going to split open like a piece of ripe fruit. I searched for my doctor's eyes, told him I couldn't do it, it was impossible, and with the next push, there was her head, outside my body. Another push and now her shoulders were free, her body sliding from me like a thing from the sea, my nine-pound prize fish.

The effort of birthing her had forced small tears in my inner labia and ripped open my perineum, both the skin and the muscle beneath.

It's a significant tear, the doctor announced somberly. But, he added, you're fortunate: you didn't tear through the anal sphincter.

I barely heard him. Purple and wailing, June was on my chest, and I prodded her upper arm gently, admiring its pudge. Brandon leaned over us, stroking my hand, which I now saw was smeared with my own blood. We studied the face we'd made. *Nine pounds!* The weight of two shrink-wrapped chickens at the grocery store. Here was the child of my body, our child, a round face with Brandon's cleft chin and dark hair. I saw on her my father's fingers, widest at their middle knuckle. Stitching me up took an hour.

Brandon and I were the first of our friends to have a baby. I'm not sure the formidable physicality of birth can be imagined, envisioned, or prepared for. The contours of motherhood only appear in their true specificity once you're inside it. Vaginal or labial tearing is extremely common, but I remember no mention of it. I might have heard something in passing, maybe in our childbirth class, but I'd never met a woman who spoke of having a tear. As far as I knew, I was alone in the wreck of my body.

We came home from the hospital when June was thirty-six hours old. Who was this—the woman in my clothes, limping through our front door, holding this baby? My perineum was swollen as a soaked sponge. Using the toilet, I was certain I would rip down the middle. *Why didn't anyone tell me?* I wondered aloud to the towels hanging on the wall. I knew I should probably look at the tear, make sure everything was healing all right. But I was too scared, so I asked my mother to do it. I never saw what it looked like.

Before June was born, we'd devised a nighttime plan. We would set up the co-sleeper on my side of the bed. We thought that made sense, because I was the one with the boobs. In the night, when she would wake, I would be able to lift her out, bring her to my chest, and feed her, both of us pleasantly half-asleep. But because of my tearing, and because learning to breastfeed is not easy, I needed help.

So we altered the plan, and in the beginning, when June woke in the night, Brandon and I both got up. He lifted her out of the co-sleeper while I wriggled out of bed. We shuffled across the hall to the nursery. He turned on the lamp and changed her while I settled into the rocking chair and positioned my various pillows. Then Brandon would place June in my arms. I'd been taught to hold my breast with one hand like a sandwich, compressed between my thumb and four fingers. I would tilt her chin toward my Dagwood sandwich and hope she'd open wide. If all went well, and it usually did after a few tries, she'd latch on and settle, and Brandon would lie down at our feet, his head on a pile of baby blankets. What I felt for him those nights was huge, vital, like its own presence, a fourth being in the nursery. I had never loved him more.

Brandon cooked in the restaurant every night it was open, five nights a week. When he needed time off, we closed the restaurant. That's what we did when I went into labor: we closed for two weeks, and for those two weeks, he took care of June and me. I was exhausted, deranged with emotion, reeling with love. Brandon was a natural parent, calm and instinctive. He knew how to hold her when she cried. He changed every single diaper. I was doing okay, all things considered. I have to remind myself of that, because I forget.

My milk came in when it should, and June was growing. But breastfeeding was painful, and week after week, it didn't stop hurting. I'd try not to let June sense my discomfort, scrambling to make small adjustments, right whatever was wrong. But I didn't know what was wrong, and no one else did, either. Everyone said breastfeeding might hurt, but not for long. Maybe my nipples just needed more time, they said, to toughen up.

The day after June was born, Brandon had given me a present, a brand-new iPad. Neither of us had used one before, and we were giddy. He'd bought it, he explained, so I could watch shows while I breastfed. One of those nights when he lay on the nursery floor, he set it up for me. It was a dumb expensive thing, but there was care behind it, sweetness and intention. I never used it. The tablet was too big to hold with one hand, and I didn't have a free hand anyway, because I needed both to hold and position June, to try to fix whatever was hurting me. I don't like to think about the iPad, the measure in aluminum and glass of the chasm between our plans and reality.

Not long after we got home from the birth, I remember sitting in our living room and imagining clearly, as though it were unspooling on the rug at my feet, a labeled timeline of my life. At one end was birth and at the other death, and in between were a series of notches, like markings on a ruler. Puberty. First Job. Lost Virginity. College Graduation. Master's Degree. Marriage. Restaurant. House. Child. As I'd made my way along the line, each notch had felt triumphant. Now I'd passed beyond "Child." This was different. This too was a triumph, but it was also, I sensed, a turn, a U-bend in the line. This notch seemed to mark a rupture, the end to some ramping-up.

I hardly remember June as a newborn. I remember my love for her like it was a room I lived in. When she was born, her eyes were late-evening blue. I remember looking at her swaddled in the crook of my arm, thinking, *This person is my child. This person will be with me when I die.* This thought made my chest ache happily, as reassuring as gravity. But a thought like that, I sensed, was only sane within the specific context of my life, with its specific history of deaths: my uncle Jerry when I was not even ten, and then on from there. My father was dead. The year after my father died, an uncle went too, his aorta exploding while he raked leaves. At twenty-five weeks pregnant, I saw my aunt Tina die. To love my baby was to be haunted. Ghosts filled the room of our love, kept us company.

I knew I probably shouldn't tell anyone about the ghosts, though it didn't feel morbid to me. I never thought of hurting my baby or myself;

that would have been something different. I found no pathology in the act of looking at my baby and thinking about death. This was grief, and grief was something I knew well. It was part of the old me, the pre-motherhood me. I was still here.

When Brandon went back to work, June was two weeks old. He was exhausted. I was too, but I was more worried about him. Since the early days of Delancey I'd had a strange emotional tic, an impulse toward panic whenever Brandon was run-down or sick. If he was out of commission, it would mean more work for me. This felt true, and sometimes it was. Of course the line of causation was never so direct, never without complicating factors. But this did not dissuade me: I should, and would, make sure Brandon was all right. New parents are famously short on sleep, but the ones I'd seen, or heard of, had been able to manage it. We would manage it. I would manage it. Other mothers were able to.

It occurs to me now that I didn't know many other mothers.

When we became parents, I needed Brandon's help. But I had trouble identifying what I needed, putting my fingertip on it. I'd had little practice. Wasn't I supposed to be a modern, independent woman? Wasn't that the idea?

And now Brandon had little to give. He was our breadwinner. Anyway, I felt lucky: even with Brandon back at work, he would usually be with us until lunchtime. He held June for hours, played music and sang.

I did ask for help with a few minor tasks, things I couldn't seem to get done on my own. I asked him to empty the dishwasher and the diaper pail, replenish the diaper stack on the shelf, and take out the garbage. I listed the tasks on a slip of paper and taped it to the kitchen cabinet. This way he wouldn't forget, and I wouldn't have to remind him.

The list helped for a few days, and then it stopped working. He said he forgot to look at it. I knew he too was tired, was struggling, overwhelmed. I knew he worried about me and June when he was at work and that he worried about work when he was with us. But I was furious that he couldn't remember a few measly chores, that he could forget my requests so easily. I was furious that he didn't notice when the tasks weren't done. I noticed, because it impacted me.

I just never think of it, he said. You know how my brain works. I just don't notice the same things you do.

I need you to start noticing, I said. I need you to try. This is *our* house. *Our* baby. I need you to do this.

But I'm already doing so much! he cried. You never notice how much I *am* doing.

I see all of it, I said. And I need more. Just for a while.

But you're better at these things, he said.

I need you to figure it out, I begged. Get good at them.

But these things are more important to you than to me. How am I supposed to remember stuff that's not important to me?

While a woman is taking care, who takes care of her? It's an earnest question: I want to know.

I wanted Brandon to care for me because I cared for him. Admittedly, it didn't always look like care. When he was worn-out, I would snap, frustrated and bitter. He was bewildered by this and rightly asked why, when he got sick, I got mean. I flailed around like Oz behind the curtain.

He *was* working hard, and I knew it. Every time we argued, we wound up here: I felt mean, cruel. I didn't want to be cruel. I didn't want to be crazy. I wanted to be reasonable. He was running Delancey and now Essex too, which was barely off the ground. We shouldn't have rushed to open it before the baby came. It had been bad advice. We had three babies: Delancey, Essex, and June.

At my six-week postpartum checkup, the doctor peered closely at my perineum.

You can hardly even see a scar, he announced. It's healed beautifully! I could hear the grin even with his face out of sight.

Elation swelled my chest. He had expected this, but I hadn't believed him. Now I lay on the exam table, heels in the cold plastic cups of the stirrups, and looked at June in her car seat on the floor, asleep in a green fleece hat. *My body*, I reeled, *did all this.*

In my senior year of college, I'd taken a class about the ethics of medical interventions, and for it I'd written an essay about my irregular periods and probable infertility. I was stunned by how little it seemed we knew about bodies, despite centuries of scientific research and study. Female bodies, in particular, remain barely within our comprehension, because the majority of studies have been on male bodies, white male bodies.[26]

I'd assumed that my body was one way, that it was empty. Now its tally of amazements was growing in plain sight.

What birth control do you plan to use? my doctor asked matter-of-factly, peeling off his gloves.

My eyes snapped to his face. Oh, I squeaked. I haven't even thought about it. Condoms?

Have you and Brandon thought about having sex? he asked. I shook my head. Well, you're healed enough now to get back to it. You can have sex anytime you'd like.

Okay, I said. I didn't expect to want it soon, but okay.

I know everything is different, he said, and that caring for a baby is hard work. But you should think about it soon—you know, get back on the horse.

Hadn't this man just been examining my injured vagina? Now we were talking about intercourse, and he was urging me to have it.

Sex is vital to a relationship, he pronounced. If it's not reestablished, the relationship can suffer. Sometimes a husband will look elsewhere.

I remember the night it started. It was November 13, 2012, and June was nine weeks old. That night she slept from seven to seven with only one waking, our best night yet. I was awake for most of it.

Sleeping as a new mother was never uncomplicated. Merely falling asleep required an assertion of willful ignorance, the ability to forget—or to not care—that I'd be up again in a couple of hours. But sleep was something that I knew how to do, and when I could get it, I took it.

That night I couldn't get back to sleep after her feeding. It was barely midnight. I studied the fuzzy edges of the halo cast by the nightlight. The bulb was the color of the pumpkins still on our front stoop. *Maybe the nightlight is keeping me up.* I rolled over. My people were breathing loudly. I reached for a pillow, pressed it over my ear. Hours passed this way. When the slits between the blinds began to lighten from black to silver, I got out of bed and tiptoed to the kitchen. There was a cottony fog blowing up the street, thick enough to obscure the house across the way. The streetlamps were still on; I watched the fog rush by them, steady as a sheet of frosted glass.

Later that morning, once Brandon was awake, I would joke about not sleeping. I didn't want to panic anyone, least of all myself. *How crazy, right, that June slept so well, the same night that I slept so little?*

That evening, in the bathroom mirror, I noticed with a start that June and I were wearing identical striped shirts. We'd worn these clothes all day, and I hadn't noticed. It was a little thing, but it unsettled me. I'd been in the bathroom with her multiple times, and it was like I hadn't been there at all.

A night of sleeplessness is normal. Difficulty is normal. I'm supposed to remember this. It's supposed to reassure me. That night, I was reassured by my own exhaustion, because when people are exhausted, they sleep. Sure enough, I fell asleep easily, as I always had. But after June's first feeding, I was again awake. *Don't rush to catastrophize*, I thought. *Difficulty is normal.*

But now every night is the same, always present tense: I am awake.

It doesn't get better with time. It gets worse. All day, I dread the night. I call the doctor. He too struggles with insomnia, he confides.

If you find yourself awake, he says, get out of bed. Don't force yourself to keep lying there. Make a cup of herbal tea, take a book to the living room. You'll sleep again soon, he says. No one can go without it for long. Remember: if you don't sleep well one night, you'll probably sleep well the next night.

I didn't. Each morning I woke up at one of the hours that's not night or day, hours familiar only to nightshift workers, cashiers in convenience stores, and mothers. I cinched the belt of my terrycloth robe, the flesh there soft and dimpled as focaccia, and shuffled to the living room to wait. June was eleven weeks old. She was sleeping the kind of long, reliable stretches we'd fantasized about two months earlier. Now I had a new fantasy: to sleep like a regular person again. During the day I'd sometimes nod off, desperate for a nap. But if I napped during the day, I'd sleep even less at night. I told Brandon that we'd made a mistake. We shouldn't have had a baby.

My doctor wrote a prescription for Ambien. I'm so sorry, he said. I took one tablet, ten milligrams, at bedtime. That first night I was hopeful, though I worried: With me drugged like this, would I hear June when she woke? I fell asleep quickly, but five hours later I was awake, without a peep from June. Before sleeping pills, at least I'd sleep until she woke me. Now there was an alarm in my bloodstream: the half-life of Ambien. Now I started to feel able to point to it: this was not normal.

"After I became a mother," writes author Sarah Manguso, "I became at once more and less lonely. I feel less lonely when I consider the nameless others, the unknown billions, who have participated in this particular loneliness."[27] I wanted to lose myself in their number. But most nights, I could imagine no other existence. Manguso again: "Whatever you're feeling, billions already have. Feel for them."[28] I couldn't get far enough outside my skull to try. Like physical pain, like a broken bone, this being-alone was inside me, with no beginning or end. No one could reach it. This is when I agreed to give it a name.

Had my doctor suggested this earlier, and I'd rejected it? Had he tried to name this problem earlier, and I'd refused to hear? It had been four weeks since I'd lost the ability to sleep. It felt like decades. I don't know.

I gave June to Brandon and went into the nursery, which was empty, to take my doctor's check-in call. I paced while we talked, my eyes grazing every object, nervous as a hummingbird. There's *Goodnight, Moon*, the well-worn copy from when I was a baby; there's the diaper pail, oh, we should empty that; there's the mobile we got off our registry, a trio of paper swallows that dart and wheel. There's the swaddle she slept in last night, a few hairs stuck in the Velcro. My doctor would phone in a prescription for Zoloft, fifty milligrams a day.

Molly, the doctor said, I know you don't believe me. But someday you will feel better. And when you feel better, you might even be glad this happened. You'll have a new kind of empathy. You'll be a different person, a person you might like.

The

Swimming

Song

17

I've been a Stevie Nicks fan since I was a kid, but it wasn't until June was born that I heard Fleetwood Mac's *Mirage*. Brandon bought it for me on vinyl, and I remember listening with June on my chest in the Ergo. When "That's Alright" came on, I cried until her hair was wet. I heard it as a sad song about love and letting go, about setting a person free and wishing them well. I thought about my new baby, about all I wanted for her, the love I hoped she would go out and find.

Now when I listen, it's obviously a breakup song. Our singer has decided to leave the person she loved. She's been thinking about it for a while, she says; this ending shouldn't surprise him.

Brandon and I are arguing again. We're arguing because we cannot stop. I wish for a megaphone. I want a way of saying *I need this* that will force him to listen. This time I will say something new.

I think I might be gay, I say.

YOU ARE NOT GAY, Brandon howls.

Even as I say it, I don't know if it's true. To say "I'm not straight" would be more accurate. But sometimes lately I feel gay. When Nora fucks me, I feel gay. On the bus, I look around at men, trying to find one I want. There are never any.

Did you not hear me? I ask. I think I might be gay.

He jerks his hands to his ears, sputtering.

You don't get to tell me who I am, I say, and I feel it all the way down, everything about me hot and bristling.

There's a tension between how a character sees herself and how others see her. I wrote that in my notes from the fiction workshop the fall after jury duty. I knew that tension. It powered me like a battery.

Now I am screaming: You don't get to tell me who I am.

We're fighting over the gristle of our marriage, and it twists and buckles in our jaws, an odd substance that won't snap. I'm tired of pleading.

For as long as we've been married, the idea of us *not* being married has seemed to me an almost physical impossibility, like walking off the edge of the earth. I couldn't imagine our marriage ending—not because of religion, not because of money, not because of children, but because of the pain. This is a good thing, I've always thought: the rupture of love *should* be unimaginable. Let's do whatever work it takes to keep it that way, to avoid an ending.

We did the work. We worked on it separately, together, and with therapists. All fights come from nonacceptance; I read this in a book, a snippet of wisdom from a Zen master. We should accept each other 100 percent. But, I want to retort, what if accepting the other person leaves you not getting what you need?

We wound up here, in this scene. Brandon stands in front of the fireplace, hands at his temples, pacing like he does when he talks on the phone. I sit at one end of the sofa, cross-legged. It takes effort to look this relaxed, to keep my voice level. I begin to explain again. I need him to hear me. I want him to understand. This time I don't want to give in.

I need you to hear me, I say, when I tell you: This is me now.

He screams something, but I can't hear it. He is far away. The effort to convince him has wrung me out. This part I do not say aloud: lately, when we argue, I wish the earth were flat, that it were really that easy to leave.

June 15, 2016. This date too will be marked on the calendar. The night before, my mother had come over after June was asleep, and we'd stayed up late talking. I told her about the arguments, about the things Brandon and I were saying to each other. My mother loves him, adores June, would never want us to fall apart. But she listened and nodded, echoed my frustration.

Am I crazy? I asked.

You're not crazy, she said. You're not crazy.

I decided that night. I had to ask for a separation. I would do it in therapy the next day, June 15. In therapy, there'd be someone to protect us from each other.

Here is how I say it: I cannot stay in our marriage. Not the way it is.

When I say it, I know immediately that I have broken something and that I won't be able to fix it, not even if I change my mind. *I have asked my husband for a separation. This is part of me now.* In the chair opposite, Brandon blinks and stares.

I'm the one I have to live with for the rest of my life, I say. Only me.

His face flattens, a mask.

I have to do right by me, I say.

Usually when we leave therapy, no matter how much we've fought, we walk out together. We stand on the balcony outside the office door and put our arms around each other. Today we will leave separately.

"I must try to get some experience," says the protagonist of Henrik Ibsen's play *A Doll's House.* A young wife and mother in late-nineteenth-century Norway, she is fed up with the narrow constraints of her life, with the feeling of being little more than a pretty doll to her husband.

"But to leave your home—your husband and your children," her husband replies. "You haven't thought of what people will say."

"I can't consider that," she says. "All I know is that this is necessary for me." She leaves their apartment as the curtain falls, slamming the door behind her.

The play raised a furor when it premiered in Copenhagen in 1879. Under protest, Ibsen rewrote the ending the following year for a production in Germany. In the altered version, the husband insists that his wife look in on their sleeping children before she leaves. He drags her to the bedroom doorway and says, "Look—there they are, sleeping peacefully and without a care," he says. "Tomorrow, when they wake and call for their mother, they will be . . . motherless!"

The young wife trembles.

"Ah, though it is a sin against myself," she cries, "I cannot leave them!" Then she collapses, and the play is over.

Ibsen would shortly declare this revised ending a "barbaric outrage," and he refused to allow its use in subsequent performances. But there it is anyway, still there, in the notes at the back of the edition at my local library: a woman talked down from the ledge of who she is.

18

A friend tells me after the fact that she was jealous of me. She's a mother of two, married to a man. *I want to blow up my life and have a lover*, she texts. *Lol?*

Lol. Nora and I are in bed, and I have asked again to go down on her. She says she doesn't come that way. Maybe I can just make you feel good, I say.

She assents. I slide down the bed, my lips tracing a line along her belly. I take my time; after all this, I'm as unsure of me as she is. I've never been here before, and I want to look at her. Her pubic hair is thick and shiny black, its borders tidy as a putting green. The skin beneath it is purplish-brown, smooth as the inside of a cheek. I want to kiss her there like a mouth, gently, a first kiss. But I know I shouldn't press my luck. So instead I begin in earnest, make my tongue flat and wide, and lap her like she's an ice-cream cone. She sighs, a small moan, and I am levitating. She permits me a half-dozen passes, maybe ten seconds, and then she starts to giggle. She swats at my head.

Not like that! She pants, her palm against my forehead. It's too ticklish! She scoots up the bed, snaps her thighs back together. She's adorable when she's got the giggles, and I hate it. I'd had my mouth on her, and she'd laughed.

I don't know how to have sex with you, I say. And I feel like you won't let me learn.

Another way of putting it, which I did not say: I am learning who you are, and this isn't working.

I wanted to touch her, move my body over hers. I wanted to play, to be allowed to play, to be pulled along, to be pushed. I wanted to take and be taken. I wanted permission to try. Instead we sat on opposite ends of the bed, not touching.

Nora leans back against the headboard. She stares at the dresser. We take turns sending out words to probe the space between us, measuring its depths.

I don't know if we're a good match, Molly, says Nora. She says my name like a threat.

I don't know what to do about this, I say. I want to say her name back to her, but it feels perilous to say it aloud, as though I've forgotten how to pronounce it.

There are a lot of ways to have sex, she says. I've had sex plenty of times without even taking my clothes off.

My head empties like a drain.

But I don't want that, I choke. I threw off all the rules to be here. I don't want a whole new set of them.

"Axiom 1: People are different from each other," writes queer theorist Eve Kosofsky Sedgwick. I imagine Sedgwick rolling her eyes at the typewriter, poking tiredly at the keys, lamenting that this should require explanation. "Even identical genital acts mean very different things to different people."[29]

Being with Nora feels like a homecoming, I wrote that summer. *But to a place I've never lived, and I can't figure out which room is mine.*

Why are there so many rules? I once asked Nora. I mean, in lots of places it's against the law for two women to have sex with each other at all. If we've already decided to break those rules, why create even more?

I had made my way to her bed because something in me had shifted. I did not choose that shift, but it had happened, and what it looked like was desire. I wanted to love and be loved by a woman. Here is the part I did choose: I followed what I wanted. Against social constraints, against my marriage, against my own instinct, against anxiety, against rules, I chose desire.

Isn't that queer sex? I wanted to ask. What is queer sex, if not a throwing-off of everything that isn't desire?

In casual conversation, one of Nora's friends referred to me as *femme*. Not in the French sense, meaning *woman* or, depending on the context, *wife*. Nora's friend called me femme as in the opposite of *butch*, as in a queer person who presents as conventionally feminine.

I remember my shock the first time I met a femme lesbian. It was at a potluck in grad school. This woman was the most mainstream-pretty of all of us, with wavy blond hair and lipstick, but that night she said something about her girlfriend, that their anniversary was coming up. It was so casual, the way she mentioned it, but she had to have known what it would signal. We'd had no clue.

Oh my god! I'd blurted. You're gay? Really? She smiled and gave a shrug. It was like witnessing a Martian landing. The year was 2002, and I was twenty-four years old. It had never occurred to me that a lesbian could look like the rest of us, that lesbians could be more than one thing, that anyone could.

Now Nora's friend called me femme. She did it in a chummy way: she was femme herself, and she was proud to claim it. I knew she meant to make me feel included, to welcome me to the club. But it didn't make me feel included. I was and have been a lot of things, none of them settled: a straight woman, a not-straight woman, a mother, a daughter, a wife in a white lace dress, a woman separated from her husband, a woman dating a woman whom some might mistake for a man. Nora's friend tried to give me language for myself, to make both of us more comfortable, but instead I felt like I'd been calf-roped.

"The mistake," writes theorist McKenzie Wark in a letter to writer Kathy Acker, "is to make a fetish of *what* differentiation produces: gay/straight; butch/femme; top/bottom, etc. Whenever these get hardened into something 'natural,' into the law, I get suspicious."[30]

Harden, like the electric-blue curing light that a dentist uses to set a newly filled cavity.

As a teenager, I wrote a lot of poetry. My father's best friend was a writer, and he gave me a couple of collections by Adrienne Rich. I don't know if I knew then that Rich was a lesbian, or if I did, it didn't mean much. But on the cusp of my thirty-seventh birthday, I took down one of the volumes and thumbed it open to "Splittings":

> I refuse these givens   the splitting
> between love and action   I am choosing
> not to suffer uselessly   and not to use her
> I choose to love   this time   for once
> with all my intelligence.

I had tried to quarantine a part of my life that frightened me. For nearly a year after jury duty, I had tried to push it away. This time I would do something different. I wouldn't leave me behind.

19

Brandon and I lived together for six weeks after I asked for a separation. We slept in the same bed, the way we'd done for a decade. We stopped fighting at home. I wouldn't do it anymore, wouldn't fight where June could hear us. We continued to fight, but in therapy.

I thought of those parachute games children play—the one where you raise your arms to lift the parachute high, as high as it'll go, and then you quickly step under it and plop down along the edge, trapping the air inside. For a moment the parachute billows above your head like a circus tent. It feels like magic, like time stops. And then, of course, the parachute starts to deflate. Our marriage was like that: the way it was built, we couldn't inhabit it. It was a structure that didn't give shelter. This sky falls if we stop holding it up.

I don't think we've been happy for a while now, I said. This isn't only about my sexuality.

I watched a wall go up in front of his face.

That's not true, he said.

I know what is true for me, I said.

We marched around and around the parachute, sizing it up.

You're trying to rewrite history, he said.

No, I'm not saying our marriage has been bad, I said. On the whole, it's been good. Our truths can be different and still valid, I said. I don't think we want the same things. I want what matters to me to matter to you, and you're allowed to want the same for yourself. We haven't been able to do that for each other.

Now you're just being mean, he said. Why are you so *mean*?

I wanted to feel that he was present. I wanted a partner in the everyday muck of domestic life, of parenting, of being a family. It was never about whether he worked nights or whether he remembered to take out the garbage; it was about feeling that he was *with me*, no matter where he was.

I think I've been lonely for a long time, I said. Have you been lonely too?

I would have done anything for you, he said. I would have given up anything. I would have sold the businesses, moved anywhere, bought a vacation house, anything. I would have done anything to make you happy.

Do you really think I could have taken you up on that? I asked. That I could have asked you to leave the restaurants, to choose a new career? Those were offers I could never cash in.

Why not?

Because you love your work. Your work *is* you. Maybe you would have given it up for me, but I would never have asked you for it.

But I would have! His voice was tight. I would have done it!

I don't want to argue anymore, I said. My eyes stung. Please stop trying to make me stay. Please stop trying to work it out. Please—just let me go.

He watched me cry.

Maybe this is dumb, he said, but do you want me to let you go in, like, two months, or do you want me to let you go right now?

I sob-laughed: I want you to let me go right now.

I got an email from the writer acquaintance whose class I'd spoken to that spring, the day I had the panic attack. She knew nothing about the intervening months. We went out for coffee to catch up. When I finished talking, she said: I don't know if this is anything, but I noticed the wording you used to describe watching the lawyer in the courtroom. You said, "I wanted to know what it was like to live in her world."

Yeah, I said, that sounds right. I'd heard myself say it before, when I told people about jury duty.

I think it's interesting, my friend said, that you put it that way. I remember when you wrote about opening Delancey, you said that you had never imagined being a part of "the restaurant world." That Brandon had chosen to enter into that world, but it wasn't really yours.

I remember that, I said. I always thought about it that way: not just as Delancey, as *his* restaurant or *our* restaurant, but as this whole world that we went into, like a separate universe with its own people and its own calendar and its own climate.

And it was never really yours, said my friend.

I did come to like it, and to be glad for it, but no.

Maybe who you are, each of you, was sort of clarified by Delancey, she said. It's like the restaurant revealed you.

Brandon moved out in the first days of August. He'd found an apartment across town, near Dino's, a large one-bedroom with a spacious walk-in closet that could be June's room. He took me to see it after he'd signed the lease. It was in a handsome brick building, with a wide spiral staircase from the lobby to the landing on the second floor, his floor. I was happy for him that he'd found a nice place. I was happy for June.

Our friends wanted to know: What had we told her? We told June that our family would now have two houses. We'd have a "Delancey house," where I lived, not far from Delancey, and a "Dino's house," Brandon's apartment. We presented this as a normal thing, a thing some families do. We said it wasn't a good thing or a bad thing, though it might be hard sometimes.

I ordered a stack of books online about separation and divorce, some for parents and some for children. The first one that came was about a family of dinosaurs who get divorced. On page five there was a drawing of a dinosaur in a pink dress and pearls, standing beside a vial of pills and tossing back a martini in one toothy gulp. The caption read, "Sometimes parents who are upset with each other behave in ways that hurt themselves and the rest of the family." I shoved the book in a bag of recycling.

From a different book in the stack I would soon learn that the strategy we'd used to present our separation to June is often referred to, scornfully, as "the real estate explanation." The complaint is that it's *not* an explanation, that it obscures what it seeks to clarify. But we didn't want to obscure the truth, I silently insisted: we wanted to be clear, and also age-appropriate. June was a month out from her fourth birthday. She didn't yet know that there was anything abnormal about her family's living arrangements. She didn't know the words *separation* or *divorce*. We would create this experience for her, and it would not be accomplished with a single conversation. We would take it one step at a time, explain with greater depth and sophistication as she lived into it, asked questions, observed. We agreed that we would not lie to her or refuse her questions. If she was sad or upset or missing one of us, we would not try to paper over it. Planning our end, we sometimes felt like a *we*.

We divvied up the furniture and June's clothes and toys. Our friends helped Brandon move. He told me he plied them with good beer. Did anyone offer a toast? I tried not to imagine what the day looked like. Brandon's parents had sent a play kitchen for June's "room" at the apartment, and my cousin shipped a box of Playmobil hand-me-downs. The apartment had old wood floors and a bank of windows at one end, and even with furniture, it echoed. I gave him two philodendrons I'd propagated the previous winter. Whenever I visited, I watered them.

There was never a question as to how we would handle custody. We would share it jointly, fifty-fifty. I had been the primary parent—had put June to bed almost every night, had bought the clothes and made the appointments and knew what was happening when—but Brandon was her father, and I knew he was a good father. He just worked a lot. He had never meant for me to be the primary parent, and now he—we—had an opportunity to change that. He wanted a fuller relationship with June, and I wanted him to have it. I wanted her to have more of him, not less. Now we had at least a shot at equal time and responsibility.

The corollary: if we were going to co-parent the way we wanted to, we would have to confront our crap. For two people who rarely did conflict well, we set lofty goals. We were both perfectionists of long standing. Brandon had spent years obsessing over making the best pizza, and I had spent years obsessing over everything.

I know it sounds dumb, he said one day in therapy, but I think we can have the perfect divorce. Then he laughed, a little too hard, so I would know he was joking. I knew he wasn't, though, not really. I rolled my eyes, but I wanted it too.

We had shimmering daydreams about how it might turn out. We said we'd hold on to what was good about our marriage, even as we undid it. We went to therapy together for a couple of months after our separation, and after that, I continued on my own. I racked up a small mountain range of credit-card debt on therapy. Our daydreams slowly lost their sheen, but we kept trying, and arguing, and trying some more. Put June first, everyone said, and she'll be okay. I hoped they were right.

When Brandon moved out, Dino's had been open for six months. He could start to pare back his hours, staying home on the nights that he had June. We planned the custody schedule accordingly and made a calendar online. We each had her three days of the week, and we alternated the remaining day. Since June wasn't used to this much time away from me, we planned the ramp-up carefully: the first week we were separated, he had June for one night; the second week, two nights; and the third week, three.

We went to the bank and opened a joint checking account for June's expenses. Our income at the time was roughly equal, so we would contribute equally to her clothes, health and dental insurance, and school costs. Whatever we bought for her that would not go back and forth—food, books, toys, an afternoon ice-cream cone—we would pay for ourselves.

Brandon and I are both white Americans from upper-middle-class families. We live in an affluent coastal city, and we both work. Our privilege made every aspect of separation and divorce—finances, custody, housing, mental health, and the list goes on—significantly easier than it is for most. According to studies of gender differences in the impact of divorce, women face disproportionate losses in household income when a marriage ends, as well as an increased risk of poverty.[31] Both parties in a divorce will deal with short-term consequences to their well-being, but the strain on women is frequently dire and lasting. My financial security—not to mention my skin color, which, because of the systemic effects of racism, underwrites much of that security—granted me agency and autonomy that few women are permitted. This truth is ugly to me, but I do not want to hide it.

I remember the night of the day that he moved out. By the light of my bedside lamp, I dug out an old T-shirt of my father's from the bottom drawer of my dresser. It was from a diner in Oklahoma City whose corned beef hash my mother once loved, royal blue cotton jersey with the restaurant's logo on the back. I'd taken it from my father's closet the year after he died, and it still smelled like him, a high-pitched musk. In thirteen years, I'd never worn it. I didn't want the smell to go away. But the day that Brandon moved out, I unfolded it and pulled it on, held the fabric to my nose until I was sobbing. I wanted company, and grief was it.

I was free from the labor of our marriage: the tidying up after him, the keeping-track, the constant doing. After he moved out, I made a mess of the place. I left dirty dishes in the sink, threw my clothes on the rug. It was a relief to stop trying to set a shining example, to stop hoping he would follow suit.

You've been begging the wrong person to see you, my therapist says. You don't have to do that anymore. I nod, not entirely sure.

Alone in our house—my house—I was defiant and furious. How had I put up with it, with how not-right we were, for so long? And then, picking up June at his apartment, I'd look around the room and nearly choke, guilt filling my mouth like a wad of gauze. June's toys were strewn everywhere, and the laundry too, and here was all this furniture that used to be ours, in this alien, half-finished place. I was the one who'd landed him here, us here, June here.

Why can't you stay married and just date girls on the side? a friend asks.

It's not like that, I say. I'm not who I was before. I couldn't be who I am and stay where I was. We tried.

I drove around a lot that summer, to Brandon's and back, to Nora's and back, to camp drop-off and back, to the restaurant and back. In the car I played the same song on repeat, "The Swimming Song," by Loudon Wainwright III. I wondered if June would remember it years later, how much I played it that summer. That summer I was always swimming, even when I wasn't. I could have drowned at any time, and often I thought I might.

If I spend enough time feeling guilty, I decided, *things will be okay. If I feel guilty enough, he will stop being angry with me.*

Three weeks into our separation, I woke up with a patch of itchy welts on my torso, the size and hue of pencil erasers. Hives. By night the spray of pink dots had joined together, the way droplets of rain make a puddle: my entire chest was covered, and my groin, my arms, the backs of my hands. Hives streaked down my legs and marched across my scalp. When June tried to climb onto my lap, I yelped. My skin pulsed and crawled, like it wanted to get away from me.

Are you allowed to grieve if you've caused the death? Is that something that can happen? I had ended my marriage, but I had also ended a life that I had, at one time, loved.

What exactly was this grief? The loss of him, of us? I wanted it to be, but I wasn't sure. We'd started to lose each other long before. I'd missed him for years. This lament was not that. *June's parents aren't together anymore*: the phrase came out of me as though someone else were speaking it, as though I were eavesdropping at the playground. I ended a life that had been not only mine, but ours.

Brandon gave me some dirt: an acquaintance had recently left his wife of two decades for another woman. We knew little of this couple and nothing of their marriage, but this feels great: the distraction of someone else's drama. I pore over the acquaintance's photos online, images and emoji-filled captions from a trip with his girlfriend. I know I am this husband, but I feel for his wife.

I think of the public radio host—a woman in her fifties, an interviewer of philosophers and poets—the one whose show I'd listened to for a long time before I learned she was divorced. When I found out, I was disenchanted. *How can she lead conversations about the meaning of human life when she doesn't even have her shit together? She can't even stay married!* As though the ability to stay in a marriage were irrefutable evidence of character, the kind of trait you might boast in a job interview. As though staying married weren't just as often motivated by fear, financial insecurity, religious codes, inertia.

The ability to leave a marriage that no longer works: What kind of character is this evidence of?

Our friends Natalie and Michael threw June a birthday party. They had a son whose birthday fell a month before hers, and for the past two years, we'd teamed up to throw a single party for both of them, halfway between the dates. This year Natalie and Michael did it all. They had a backyard barbecue one weekend afternoon in mid-August, with a tent full of balloons and a plastic kiddie pool. I don't remember much except how hot it was outside. I remember watching Natalie and Michael, thinking how easy they made it look, thinking, *Their son will grow up with both of his biological parents under the same roof.*

A friend was in town from New Orleans that weekend, someone Brandon knew better than I did. This friend was a photographer, and he took a picture of Brandon and June at the birthday party. In it they were laughing, their cheeks flushed with heat. I noticed that our friend did not take a picture of me. I spent most of the afternoon sitting by myself in Natalie and Michael's dining room, trying not to notice anything at all.

20

Nora had a nephew and two nieces. They were her brother's children, and they lived on the East Coast. She told me about them on our first date, said she loved kids. She wanted to know: What was June like? What were her favorite toys? What did June know about where I was, on nights like these? Nora was eager to meet her and appropriately nervous. She deferred to my sense of timing, and I was grateful for that. I didn't know what to do. I needed time to figure it out.

Nora met June a couple of weeks after Brandon moved out. She came over for dinner, and I made soup. Nora had brought June a hamburger stuffie the size of a hatbox, and June was thrilled. Nora watched us quietly. I explained to June that Nora was a new friend, but that night she didn't seem like a friend, or like my girlfriend. It seemed like she'd never met a child before, like she'd showed up for dinner at the wrong house. We were all terrified.

I was a mother, but I felt like a virgin—an identity with notable precedent, but not what I was going for. I wished I were more like Athena, fully formed from the get-go. My life had so many *complications*: that was the word that came to me. My life was ungainly, unwieldy. Surely it was impossible to love. If I could barely handle it, how on earth could Nora?

Nora told me she felt like a homewrecker. Am I? she asked.

No, no—you're absolutely not, I said. I'm leaving my marriage for me, I said. No one is responsible but me.

I met her mother once. She was visiting from the East Coast, and she wanted to meet me. She offered to take us to dinner, chose a steak restaurant. I liked the idea of being brought into the fold, and I dressed up for the evening. Nora's mother asked about June. She asked about my mother. She couldn't wait to know them. The next afternoon, we all met up at a playground. Nora's mother had stopped at a toy store and lavished June with gifts, a brand-new flower-print backpack full of them. She was trying hard, and it touched me. June was reticent, quiet in her excitement. She had no idea who this woman was, and I barely did either.

June didn't want me to talk with the other grown-ups; she wanted me to join her on the playground equipment. Nora hung back with our mothers, made periodic visits to me and June on the swings. I wanted her to stay with us, to join us in our play, swing high like we did. She leaned on the steel supports, hands in her pockets, and stared out at the lake. She walked with our mothers down to the water. I dragged June's doll and new backpack over the grass toward them, sweating and irritated and sad. None of us knew what to do in this scene.

Recently my mother reminded me about that afternoon. God, remember that? Doesn't it seem like ages ago? She thought we could laugh together about its awkwardness. Instead I cringed. I had wanted things to work out with Nora, wanted it enough to introduce our parents. But it hadn't worked—not that afternoon, not really anytime.

"The trouble with letting people see you at your worst," writes Sarah Manguso, "isn't that they'll remember; it's that you'll remember."[32]

Brandon and Nora met only once, the morning of Labor Day. She had come over for dinner the night before, and he texted early, while we were still in bed. He wanted to grab a tool from the garage. Nora's here, I replied, but you can come if you want. She says she'd be happy to meet you.

He arrived with June in tow. Surely it couldn't have happened any other way but this: on short notice, so no one had time to get anxious, and with June around, a healthy distraction. He knocked, and I answered, Nora waiting in the hall. Brandon bounded in, extending his hand. I could see the effort behind his high spirits, and a tender sting rose in the back of my throat. When I walked him and June out to the car, his eyes were wet, unspeakable.

21

One Monday, I was at the restaurant, calculating tips for payroll. June was at the dance studio next door, taking her first pre-ballet class. Brandon was in the kitchen, doing prep for the next day. It was late September.

Do you have time to make a vanilla ice-cream base? he asked. I did. I found the milk and cream in the walk-in, cracked the eggs. At his station, Brandon chopped shallots for vinaigrette. June's class ended, and she sat at the counter in her gossamer skirt with a blanket tied around her shoulders. It was like old times, old times we'd never really had.

On the stereo, the first notes of an Elvis Perkins album kicked in. It was one of a dozen songs I associate with the opening of Delancey, songs we listened to over and over. We'd listened as we poured the concrete tabletops and painted the ceiling, as we polished silver and stacked plates, the two of us hacking away at a project that I wished I'd wanted. *Elvis Perkins in Dearland* had become the soundtrack of that feeling, a preemptive nostalgia as one phase of our lives slid into the next. For years after Delancey opened, when I needed a good cry, I'd play that album like a musical ipecac, to shake loose and expel a feeling.

Now, this Monday afternoon, Brandon put it on the stereo. *So he noticed too*, I thought, the way this afternoon was a kind of echo, an ideal echo, of times we'd had before.

Stop, stop! I begged, grinning. Turn it off, or I'll cry! Don't make me do it!

We laughed, and he put on something else. I could hear that laugh for hours. It was a relief to recognize who we'd been to each other and to not pretend we were still the same.

Nora and I talked on the phone on the nights when we didn't see each other. That night I wanted to tell her about the afternoon at Delancey, but I hesitated. I worried that it wouldn't land right. But she'd wanted to know about my day, hadn't she? I wanted to be able to tell her about the things that matter to me. So I told her about it.

Gosh, she said. It's kind of hard to hear that.

Why? I asked. I'd play dumb.

Sometimes it seems like you're going to get back together, she said.

He's the father of my child, I said. I want a good relationship with him. That's not the same as wanting to stay married to him. You can understand that, right?

It's just hard to hear about the two of you together, Nora said.

Something hot surged in the back of my throat. I had brought her a positive event, but to her it wasn't good news. I had come to her with light; she took it in and became something dark.

When clouds of space dust form so densely that light rays cannot pass through, they appear in the night sky as black patches, shapes even darker than midnight. Astronomers call them dark cloud constellations.

I've got to be able to talk about my life, I said, without us falling apart over it.

When Nora and I talked, I didn't like who I became. Every conversation was a mirror, and I didn't like the person I saw in it. This person wriggles uncomfortably in her seat, can't seem to stay here or there. This person can't do it right. She wants the wrong things.

One version of the right thing: this person should have stayed in her marriage. She should have held fast to her commitment. She should have thought of her child first—her child's need for security, consistency, an intact home.

Another version of the right thing: this person should have left like a snake sheds its skin. She wanted to be free, right? Wipe off the dust and go.

Interview your character. Ask her what she wants.

"But now," writes author Andrea Long Chu, "you begin to see the problem with desire: we rarely want the things we should."[33]

This person wants neither.

Being with Nora was like riding a teeter-totter with someone much smaller or much larger than you are. This is what I tell my friend Matthew. Nora and I were always each at the mercy of the other, either floating up or thudding down, never at the same time. We were both afraid of being left up there.

I think I'm homesick, I say to Matthew. It's like I can't get comfortable anywhere. It's like I'm homesick for a comfort I don't have anymore.

He nods.

I can't stay in my marriage, I say, but I don't want to burn it to the ground either.

No one says you have to, he says.

I have this daydream, I say. It's me and Brandon, a couple of years from now. We're sitting in the shade somewhere. We're talking, maybe eating something. We're just two friends, normal friends, catching up.

From the corner of my eye I see Matthew's lip curl into a mild smile. I amuse him.

I know it sounds dumb, I say. Like I'll burst into song and Brandon'll do a tap dance and then the credits will roll.

Ha, Matthew blurts. It does, a little.

But I really want us to get there.

You maybe can do it someday, says Matthew. But it'll be a lot of work.

I know.

Well, he says, then go do it.

22

The next day was a Wednesday, still late September. Brandon and I had a meeting with our CPA, and then with a corporate attorney. We had to decide what to do with the restaurants, whether we would continue to own them jointly. Between meetings, we got falafel for lunch and leaned against his car to eat it. It was windy, and I was wearing a blue skirt, I remember, because it was whipping around my calves when he said that he could see it now, that we hadn't been real partners, romantic partners, for a long time. Maybe not since he moved from New York. We've just been best friends, he said.

I nodded, swallowing.

I've missed my friend, he said.

Me too, I said. I couldn't look at him, not sure of what my face would do. I watched a bee crawl along the curb.

I made a list last night of everything I need in our relationship, he said. And I think it's probably impossible to fix it all. It would make us both miserable.

I think so too, I said. I could feel the molecules between us rearranging themselves.

Nora met me like an enzyme, and she catalyzed a reaction. Now I studied the fine print. *Catalyst*: a substance that increases the rate of a chemical reaction without itself undergoing any permanent chemical change.[34]

In our reaction, I was the one changing. That was never her role.

*

I asked Nora to meet me that afternoon on a bench in the park where we'd had our first date. I said I couldn't do it anymore. I was livid and empty, like a blister that's been popped. I said I couldn't be with someone who didn't actively support—support and encourage—my having a good relationship with the father of my child.

But I do, she said. I do.

Maybe you do, I said, but I can't feel it. That time in bed, when you said maybe we weren't a good match, I think you were right. I looked at her face, the red of her eyes. I'm sorry, I said. You were right.

My mouth was dry, like moving my tongue around a cardboard box. As we said goodbye, a breeze picked up the dead leaves at our feet and threw a lock of hair against my front teeth, where it stuck.

Back at my car, I found a crater in the windshield, a dense web of cracks with fissures running in all directions. I spun around, looking for Nora, but she'd left by a different exit. She wouldn't have done this anyway. There was a faint smear at the center of the crater, as though a bird had hit it, or a dusty baseball. The point of impact was directly in front of the driver's seat. I swept the flecks of glass from my seat and drove home.

23

Now I took the dog out before bed, a chore Brandon used to do. Each night, while she did her thing, I studied the sky. I would see how far up and behind I could look before I staggered backward on my heels. The rainy season had begun, and most nights there were no stars. But when it was clear enough, I'd look for Orion's Belt, follow it to Sirius, then back the other way to the Pleiades. I measured time that way, one day into the next, one month into the next, watching the giant hunter stride across the sky.

Before that fall, I had never lived in our house alone, as its sole adult resident. Brandon and I had had big plans for the house, but we hadn't had the money to see them through. He'd left without complaint. You know me, he said. I'll have fun finding a new house someday. You know I like a project.

I threw out his expired prescriptions and the ominous-looking earwax-removal kit he'd never used. I got tired of seeing the garden hose lolling next to the driveway like a diseased reptile, so I went to Fred Meyer and spent $29.99 on a plastic caddy on wheels. No one has so triumphantly coiled a hose.

While I futzed, I listened to podcasts. In an episode of *On Being*, Krista Tippett mused with Franciscan friar Richard Rohr on the nature and necessity of suffering. It's a simplistic metaphor, Father Rohr explains, but, "Picture three boxes: order, disorder, reorder. . . . If you read the great myths of the world and the great religions, that's the normal path of transformation. What I always tell the folks is there's no nonstop flight from order to reorder. . . . Yeah, that disorder is part of the deal."[35]

This was around the time that the sewer backed up onto the old cherry-red carpet of the basement bathroom. The sewer pipes under the yard had eroded and split and would have to be replaced, at substantial cost. This work would not be covered by homeowners' insurance. Because we still owned the house jointly, Brandon and I split the bill, both pillaging our savings. I cried a lot, made calls to a contractor acquaintance, and scoured Yelp reviews of sewer companies. Water mitigation, asbestos abatement, trenchless sewer replacement: I would learn to use these terms correctly in a sentence.

I sat in bed one night and wrote a list of people who had been kind to me in the previous year. I wondered why they had. I wondered if I deserved it. I wondered what I did deserve, after what I had done. I had developed a feverish obsession with someone who was not my spouse; had ended my marriage of a decade, thereby stripping my child of a home with both her parents in it; and had meanwhile spent five months riding the chaotic sea of a relationship that sent me pitching with lust, self-loathing, and confusion, in that order, only to end it. I felt bruised and embarrassed, and unsure of how else I could have done it. At any given moment, I had acted the only way I knew to act. At any given moment, I knew only what I knew. The limits of my judgment, of my own good sense, humiliated me.

When June makes mistakes, my therapist observed, you don't stop loving her, do you? Even when she acts in a way you don't like, you never assume she's "bad." You separate her actions from the essence of who she is. What if you could do that for yourself?

But did I deserve it?

One afternoon while June was in school, Brandon came over to pick up something, and when he walked into the living room, he burst into tears. He threw himself face-first onto the sofa and wailed. He was taller than the sofa was long, so his sneakered feet hung off one end, shaking with each sob. I didn't know what to do, so I went into the kitchen and started to scrub at a smear of something on the counter. I wanted him to leave, to go do it somewhere else.

Did I deserve love? Did I deserve pleasure?

I wanted to learn how to date. Compared to women I knew, I had dated little in the years before I married. Mostly I was in a relationship, or I was not.

I just wanted practice. I needed practice at being whatever I was. I didn't want to think about love. I wanted to be fucking someone.

A friend pressed into my hands a copy of Maggie Nelson's *The Argonauts*, and I covered it with Post-it flags. "I can remember, early on," Nelson writes, "standing beside you . . . completely naked, . . . as you asked me to say aloud what I wanted you to do to me. My whole body struggled to summon any utterable phrase. I knew you were a good animal, but felt myself to be standing before an enormous mountain, a lifetime of unwillingness to claim what I wanted, to ask for it."[36]

I wanted to live on my own terms. My terms were this: I was a newly queer woman and also a mother.

Separated with fifty-fifty custody, I was set loose for half of each week, my tether reeled out as far as it could go. I knew I shouldn't tell my married friends with full-time children how great this was; that would be cruel. I had a feeling I shouldn't tell anyone how much I liked being a childless mother. As a mother, I was supposed to grieve every hour I was without my child.

I got half of my own life back, with the added perspective of parenthood to throw it into brilliant relief. I could see what I had and appreciate it. And I would have to hang on tight to that feeling when it shimmered over me, because each time June cried and clung to me as I buckled her into Brandon's car, each time she asked why we had to have two houses, I knew I was the cause of her grief.

On an episode of *Dear Sugar*, Cheryl Strayed posits that wanting to leave a relationship is enough reason to do it. You have to be brave enough to break your own heart, she says. What about my child's heart? I want to shoot back: What if I break that too?

When I was a teenager in my parents' house, there was a chair in front of my bedroom window, but I never used it. The only time I remember sitting there was the day before I left for college, as I folded a pile of clean laundry. My father stood in the doorway of my room, one shoulder against the frame, keeping me company while I packed. I was tired and on edge, anxious about leaving, though I wouldn't say it out loud. Instead I heaved a series of showy sighs.

How're you holding up? my father asked, taking the bait.

This is too hard, I moaned. There's too much to do.

You mean packing? he asked. But you're almost done.

I mean everything. I don't know how I'm supposed to do this! I slumped over my thighs, really going for it.

Now his voice came out stony and strange: You'd better get used to it, he said. This is how it is. Life is hard.

The change was so abrupt, I thought surely he was ribbing me. A humming quiet filled the air. I looked up, expecting a smile. Instead he shoved off the doorjamb, walked across the hall, and shut his door.

I was about to turn nineteen, and I had a plane ticket to Northern California, where I would in theory start my life. My father was sixty-eight. He was in good health, though probably, unbeknownst to all of us, carrying around the cache of faulty cells that would kill him five years later. He was still seeing patients in his oncology practice, living in the house that he and my mother had always dreamed of. He was happy. But the man wasn't young. Born in 1929, my father was the oldest son of a family of Jews who'd recently immigrated from Poland to Canada. As a teenager, he watched the Holocaust from an ocean away, witnessed the German government kill six million people like him, including his extended family. He dragged around all the aches, sorrows, and piles of personal garbage that a human accumulates over seven decades of living. When *Schindler's List* came out, he took me to see it. Afterward, in the orange light of the cinema hallway, I noticed that his eyes were a paler shade of blue than normal, like shallow seawater. He was crying. That was the only film I ever went to with him; he said he didn't like going to the movies.

The thing he said that day in my doorway stayed with me. I wondered at it sometimes, tugged at it like one of June's tiny hair ties in my pocket. What would he say to me now? About Brandon, about my falling in love with a woman, about divorce, or climate change, white nationalism, bump stocks, the audacity of Donald Trump running for president? Given everything—my life as it now looks and the world we live in, the abyss of which my father seemed to peer down that day—do we get to be happy? How often?

I want to know what he would say about June, in whose face I now find his eyes. I want to know what he would say about the mess I've made of her family, about how to help her survive it, about how to be her mother and also myself. I want to know if my father would tell me what I have begun to suspect: that I couldn't have done any of this without her.

I think a seismic shift started in me, millimeter by millimeter, when June was born. Having a baby, having her, softened me. It broke me a little. It gave me intimate knowledge of the emptiness that is clinical depression, and it also gave me access, on the other side, to a rounder fullness of joy. Having her made me value my body, and femaleness, in a new way. Becoming her mother grew me up. It committed me to becoming the kind of person I want her to know, remember, be proud of. It committed me to becoming the person I want her to have as a parent.

The

Pink

Fish

24

In October, we drove east to go apple-picking. Friends had chosen an orchard from a list online and invited us to come along. We took my car: me, Brandon, June, and my mother. But when we got there the apples were picked over, and those that remained were covered in brown scabs and scales. June began to pout, stomping around with an empty basket. I wanted to leave everyone by the side of the road, go home and back to bed.

In an attempt to recover the afternoon, someone suggested a picnic. We found a spot by a river nearby. I cut slices of salami and managed to chase the kids around, and June's spirits rose. Her cheeks were pink in the cool air, and for once, she didn't trip or fall down or skin some body part or other. We played hide-and-seek behind a stand of wilting anemones. But I stayed vaguely grouchy all day, outside of myself, as though my skin were too tight. I glared at our friends, the couple who'd hosted June's birthday party two months earlier. They were so good, their marriage purring along like a sleek new coupe in a car commercial. I wanted to be with my own people, whoever they were.

The last winter that Brandon and I were together, three couple-friends came to us with a proposal for a new tradition: What if, one night of each week, our four families got together for dinner? We'd rotate houses, each only hosting one out of four weeks. It might be a lot of work, but we'd be building a chosen family of sorts, an extended family for our kids. Once a week seemed ambitious—and potentially overwhelming for me, an introvert of long standing—but I wanted it for June. It might be good for all of us.

We kept at it after the separation, adding a fifth house—Brandon's apartment—to the rotation. I loved and hated Thursdays. One family had begun renovating a house. Another was pregnant again. These families were making steady forward progress, while mine had slipped off track. We were moving backward. *You're not seeing the whole picture here*, I tried to coax; *you have no idea, not really, what other people's marriages are like.* But watching my friends' families blossom brought pain as real as a headache.

I thought of a friend who, after her young business fell apart, had disappeared from our lives. We'd known each other through a lot, including the opening of Delancey. But when her own project ran aground, though we had no connection to it, she cut us off, along with most of her friends from that period of time. Brandon and I were miffed: She *divorced* us! Now, at the Thursday night dinner table, I could hazard a guess why: it must have been hard enough to struggle as our friend had, but to let us *see* her struggle would have been worse.

"Theirs is a happy marriage, a joint creation of great delicacy and skill," writes Rachel Cusk in *Aftermath*, a memoir of her divorce. "I have always admired it, have liked to look at it and be in its presence. . . . But things are different for me now. My admiration has become a kind of voyeurism. . . . I'm not equal any more with the people I know, and what is friendship but a celebration of equality?"[37]

I saw endings everywhere. As I read aloud to June from Mo Willems's *Goldilocks and the Three Dinosaurs*, the end of the book winked with a moral: "If you ever find yourself in the wrong story, leave."

About six weeks after Brandon moved out, I was keeping June company in the bathroom one evening when she asked what happens when we die.

I don't know, I admitted. I took a breath. Maybe anything we want can happen? We won't have our bodies anymore, so we could probably do whatever we want, I said. Maybe we can fly like birds or swim like fish.

What do you want to do? June asked.

I think I might want to fly, I said.

I want to be a fish! she said, sitting up straighter on the toilet seat. I'll be a pink fish! And you'll be a pink fish too. And Daddy will be a purple fish.

I lowered myself onto the wooden stool that my second cousin had given us when June was born, with her name and birthdate spelled out in puzzle letters.

We'll all swim around together. Right, Mama? She looked at me, waiting. I nodded, not sure if I was happy, or sad, or some third thing.

We swapped June on Mondays usually, sometimes Tuesdays. The first day without her was disorienting, as though I'd misplaced something terribly important, left my wallet at the store. But now I had time, gaping stretches of time, wide-open rolling meadows of it.

I searched online for information about sexual orientation in women, trying to understand what had happened to me. One book kept coming up, so I ordered it. It was called *Sexual Fluidity: Understanding Women's Love and Desire*, by a psychologist named Lisa M. Diamond. When it arrived, I put it on my bedside table. Then I piled a bunch of other books on top of it. I caught up on the *New Yorker*. I went to IKEA, bought June a big-girl bed and assembled it. I started my first quilt. I'd learned to sew a couple of years earlier, when Brandon bought me a sewing machine for Christmas. Now with evenings to myself, I drank beer and watched YouTube videos with titles like "How to Stitch in the Ditch" and "Easy Improv Quilting." I splashed around in my free time like it was an Olympic-size pool, all to myself.

While prying loose a clump of dog hair stuck under a baseboard in the front hall, I got a splinter under my fingernail. The splinter was tiny, but I couldn't get it out, and it leaked pus when I pressed on the nail. I called the doctor's office, got a last-minute appointment with a nurse. Waiting in the exam room, I noticed the cover of a magazine on the chair beside me. It was a giant photo of a beaming Hollywood blonde, and next to her face, hot-pink letters shouted: 45 AND SINGLE! AND FEELING GREAT!

Along came a fresh kind of dread. I took a picture of the cover and texted it to Matthew.

Is this going to be me? I wrote.

You'll meet someone, he replied.

How? Where?

Anywhere, he says. *You met Nora in a* courtroom.

On the mirror above the bathroom sink I stuck two columns of Post-it notes, reminders of things June and I were working on.

June's notes, in carnation pink:

PEE BEFORE BED
BRUSH 2x / FLOSS
THUMB-SUCKING

My notes, in light blue:

BE CURIOUS
BE PATIENT
THE MISTAKE IS NOT IMPORTANT; THE WAY
    YOU RECOVER IS
"YOU HAVE TO BE WILLING TO BE BAD AT IT IN
    ORDER TO GET GOOD AT IT"

The last was a quote I'd pulled from the book *In the Company of Women*. It was from an entrepreneur named Mary Going, intended as advice about work and business. When I stuck it to the mirror, I was mostly thinking of going down on a woman.

Out one day, I ran into a friend of a friend. She was easy to talk to, and I mentioned my separation.

Do you have any friends who are divorced? she asked. I'll be your divorced friend.

We made plans to go out for drinks a couple of weeks later. Over a plate of nachos, we traded stories. I recounted the tale of Nora, said I now wanted to date casually, full stop—*caaaasually*, I enunciated. She asked if I had "a type."

I like androgyny, I said, my first time saying it aloud. I'm attracted to both men and women, but really I like people who aren't exactly either.

What word do you use for yourself, for your orientation? she asked. Do you use *queer*?

I guess, I said. Maybe *bisexual* works. But I don't just want it both ways; I want it *every* way. I fished an ice cube from my margarita and crunched on it. I've never been into, like, American-man men. No men-men. I loved that Brandon was a composer. He threw dinner parties in college, you know?

Ha, she said. I didn't know that.

I think I like softer men, I said, and harder women. I liked how this sounded in my mouth.

I might know someone you'd be into, said my friend. She gave a smile, quick and devious, and grabbed her phone. Scrolling through somewhere, she produced a photo. It was grainy, with the ersatz orange haze of an iPhone filter, but in it was a fine-boned girl with very short dark hair, sitting in what looked like a swiveling desk chair. She was beautiful, but not like a girl. She looked like the lead singer of a boy band.

Oh, I snorted. Yeah, I'd totally fuck her.

Her name is Ash, my friend said. I used to work with her at my old job. Want me to see if I can set you up?

We went out on a Thursday night. It was raining hard for Seattle, a hood-up kind of rain, and I got to the bar first, glad for a second to rearrange my bangs. I was too antsy to sit down in a booth, so I stood at the bar and made small talk with the bartender. He was the same one who'd bought me and Nora a round on our first date, but at a different bar. I tried not to read into it. At the edge of my vision I saw Ash walk in and felt my heartbeat thud, *ca-su-al*, down the length of my arms.

She was twenty-nine. When I told her I was thirty-eight, it felt like a dare. Her last girlfriend, she smiled, was thirty-nine. We fiddled with the straws in our drinks, stayed for two hours, walked around the corner for Malaysian food. She'd come out a few years ago, she said; like me, she'd felt straight before that. Then a year ago she came out again, this time as non-binary, gender-nonconforming. I liked how easily she said it. When she turned to speak to the server, I gawped at her: the line of her jaw, angular and delicate, and the confident slash of her brow. At each corner of her mouth a soft crease ran perpendicular to her lips, and it gave a tiny fullness to the flesh there. I wanted to suck on it. We closed down the restaurant and walked out to my car. The rain had let up, and she handed me the paper bag of leftovers. The street was busy, cars sluicing us with rainwater as they sped by. Can I walk you to your car? I asked, depositing the leftovers on the seat. She pointed us up a side street and we went, shoulders knocking through our coats. I couldn't look at her. When we got to her car it was raining again. There was a slope to the sidewalk, and I was below her, which was perfect, because now we were the same height. I asked if I could kiss her. We both started to giggle, shy now, and she put her lips on mine. I opened my mouth to her, searched out her narrow hips under my hands. I could feel her start to smile as I kissed her, and I pulled her closer, flicked my tongue along the inside of her cheek. I liked the taste of her mouth, like fried rice and clean water. The rain was coming down steadily, ice-cold on the back of my neck, and the nylon of our raincoats scritched-scritched. Can I see you again? she asked, and I said, Please. I pressed my pelvis against her. She whispered into my teeth, threw her head back, and laughed, did a giddy soft-shoe. I wanted her to be more aloof, hot and distant—a gun for hire, for sex. I wished she liked me less.

When we were soaked, she offered to drive me back to my car. We clambered into hers, and the windshield wipers squeaked to life. Heat blasted from the dash, and I rubbed my hands in front of the vent. When she pulled up behind my car, I found I didn't want to get out. I looked at her, and she turned in her seat, and like horses we nuzzled, touched our faces cheek to cheek.

I'd told the friend who set us up that I didn't want anything big. Maybe one night a week, I said, and waved my index finger for emphasis. I learned on our first date that Ash had low bandwidth too: she worked full-time with a long commute. I was glad to hear it. I wanted to be dating, but I didn't want to give up my time. I didn't want to cede the very tentative feeling that I would be all right on my own, that June and I would make it.

I keep a picture of me and June framed in the hallway outside the bathroom. It was taken right around that time, on a Sunday morning at the neighborhood farmers' market. Our dog, Alice, was with us on her leash. While I was picking out apples at one of the farm stands, a smartly dressed man with a vintage Polaroid camera approached, offering to take our picture for a few dollars. I felt spontaneous, said yes. June and I sat on the curb and positioned Alice beside us. June wears a pale blue unicorn-print raincoat over her Snoopy pajamas, and she's eating from a small tub of Greek yogurt. She squints at the camera, smiles, chews on the spoon. Alice, never one for eye contact, looks off down the street. My hair is long in this photo, almost to my breasts, and it looks golden against the black collar of my coat. I look content. I look at ease, maybe more than I'd ever seen myself.

Here's a glaring example of confirmation bias, but I like it: "Nothing," asserts psychiatrist Carl Jung, "exerts a stronger psychic effect upon the human environment, and especially upon children, than the life which the parents have not lived."[38]

25

When Brandon and I separated, I had not yet come out to most of my family. I'd come out to a couple dozen friends and colleagues, mostly people I saw regularly and couldn't hide from. I had come out to my mother in the emergency room and to a cousin who'd visited that summer, but not to anyone else. That fall, I made a list of the people left to tell. I did most of the calls in my car, on speakerphone, on days when I didn't have June. Each call would have a predictable and finite duration, like a college exam. I would give each the length of time it took to get where I was going: from home to Delancey, the mechanic to the grocery store, Delancey to a meeting at June's school.

My family was kind. I knew the conversation wasn't easy for anyone in it. But I hated the questions they asked me, the fact that they thought they could. One asked how Brandon was doing "with it all." I seethed, though the question was understandable. Brandon's okay, I said; we still care a lot for each other. All I can say, replied my family member, is that Brandon is an unusually good man.

When I was straight, I did not have to come out. Like my white skin, my being straight was a convenient default. There was a nice slip to it, an absence of friction. There was also privacy: when straight, I rarely had to disclose anything about my sex life. Even pregnancy, the visible fact of a baby protruding from my abdomen, unavoidable evidence of sexual activity, didn't say anything about my sexuality. Only those who don't fit norms have to put a name to their difference. The world has gay politicians and legal same-sex marriage, but there is still a thing called coming out. Now there would be endless occasions to out myself, whether I wanted to or not. Like at my dermatologist's office one afternoon, when he inquired about my preferred method of birth control.

Oh, I don't need any, I said.

Why not? he asked, swiveling abruptly from his computer and peering at me over his reading glasses.

I'm dating a woman, I said.

Ah! He laughed, visibly relieved. He'd worried that I would extoll the virtues of the rhythm method or prayer. I was glad for his mirth. I wondered how this conversation might go in a less progressive town.

I knew I was fortunate to have other concerns. I was afraid people would think I'd been hiding it, that I'd been faking my way through life. I was afraid people would think that everything I'd been and done was a lie. I had written two memoirs featuring Brandon, our courtship, and our marriage. I built my career as a writer on a certain image, because that image had been true. But now the story I have to tell seems to undo all the ones that came before, the ones people have come to know me by. How does a person write truthfully about their life, when it isn't finished?

I wanted to be believed, though I struggled to explain myself. And if they—family, friends, readers—did believe me, wasn't it almost worse? Then they'd see me as some kind of a contagious illness, something they or their spouses could catch. I'd seen the thought pass over friends' faces as I spoke. I was a harbinger of unwelcome news: *Look out, straight people! This could happen to you AT ANY TIME.* On a weekend getaway, a friend confessed to me that her husband had joked that she would "go off into the woods with Molly and come back gay." We both laughed. What else was I supposed to do.

Another family member asked how my mother was "holding up." Oh, she's amazing, I fumbled. I explained that I knew how hard it must have been for her, especially since she'd only recently moved to town. I was grateful for the work she was doing to accept and understand and be there for me—for all three of us.

Well, this family member scoffed, you've really put her through the wringer, Molly.

This time I had the gall to attempt a protest. Excuse me? I howled. But that's not to imply that I didn't agree.

*

Saying that my husband and I had separated was worse than coming out. I couldn't just say it; I was sure I should explain. Our separation was my fault, and I would announce this culpability by outing myself. On three occasions, I outed myself to staff members of June's school. I hardly knew any of them. I saw their heads wobble faintly with the impact, watched them labor to respond. It seemed easier to pawn my privacy, to flay myself next to the playground sandbox, than to let someone make assumptions. Then they might land on the tender thing: my marriage hadn't worked very well.

When did I stop loving Brandon? Did I? Why would I even formulate such a question, as though it mattered in the end? "There are some people that one loves," admits the wife in Ibsen's *A Doll's House*, "and others that one perhaps would rather be with."

26

Ash and I went on a second date, this time to a movie. I was running late, and I texted to say she should go ahead and get seats. I shimmied into the theater as the lights started to dim, hoped she couldn't see how I blushed when I saw her. I sat down, and she leaned close: Are you a hand-holder? I nodded, and she put her elbow on the armrest, opened her palm. Her skin was smooth and even, like a new ream of paper. After the movie we went for tacos and made out standing against the back hatch of my car. I rubbed the seam at the crotch of her jeans, pinched her lip in my teeth, let the rear wiper dig into my back.

The morning was overcast, and I sent Ash a text: *Today is prime makeout weather.*

It IS, she replied. *I can't wait to make out with you again.*

I'm currently making granola, I typed back. *This is what it's like to sext with me. I'm also listening to a feminist podcast about menstrual cups.*

Hubba hubba, typed Ash. *I haven't had my period in almost a year.*

A beat, then she added: *Not for any unhealthy reasons, thankfully.*

Oh, why not? I asked.

About a year ago, she replied, *my doctor and I decided that a very low dose of testosterone might help me feel more aligned with my gender identity, which is queer/non-binary. Does that freak you out?*

Not at all! I hope you didn't feel on the spot. It must be wild to experience that kind of deep change in yourself.

I didn't feel on the spot, she said. *It felt like a good way to drop that into the convo. And yes, it has been wild. I'm amazed at how much more myself I feel. I started sleeping better, feeling happier. There is growing evidence of lowered rates of depression and anxiety with hormone therapy, though most research is based on folks who are taking a dose to fully transition. The stress of living incongruent to one's gender identity can be so harmful.*

I'm really glad for you, I said.

People are still learning, Ash added. *Myself included. The world still operates by a "this or that" framework. Even my doctor uses language implying that because I am on hormones, I want to transition. Which is wrong.*

I typed: *There's this really great passage from a book I love, The Argonauts, by Maggie Nelson. "How does one get across the fact that the best way to find out how people feel about their gender or their sexuality—or anything else, really—is to listen to what they tell you, and to try to treat them accordingly, without shellacking over their version of reality with yours?"*

I couldn't yet tell her what the quote meant in my story. I couldn't yet tell her about the times my husband had said I was crazy, about the time he'd tried to tell me I wasn't gay and I'd wanted to scream this at him, every word.

On our third date I was looking down, fiddling with my phone, when Ash arrived. She slid onto the booth beside me like an apparition, and when I turned to see why the light had changed, her face was close to mine. I put my tongue in her mouth.

I've never asked about your pronouns, I said. I just realized it. I'm sorry I didn't think to earlier.

That's fine, she said. I've been thinking about it lately. It's kind of a shifting thing. I've just started using they/them at work, and it feels really good. So, they/them, I think.

Okay, I said, great. I can do that.

I had quietly hoped that I could keep saying "she/her." But even as I thought it, I felt bad. *Ash's pronouns have nothing to do with me. I should be happy to call them whatever they want.* The singular "they" felt strange on my lips, like practicing a new language. But I could practice, and I wanted to.

We were supposed to see *Moonlight*, but we lost track of time. There was a Halloween party at Dino's, and we stopped by. Brandon was there with someone he'd been seeing. I hugged him en route to the dance floor, and his date whispered in my ear: You two look so beautiful. Ash is like a tiny shiny Bieber lady.

When I told Ash, I could see them flush under the low purple lights. You know I've dressed as Justin Bieber for Halloween, they confessed. Three times.

Ash pulled up a split-screen picture on their phone: Bieber on the left, Ash-as-Bieber on the right. It was perfect. I cackled, doubled over.

We walked to the car with our arms around each other. It was late, but there were lots of bars on this street, and people outside them to smoke. We were safe: this was the gay part of town, the urban gut of Seattle, where bass thumps from the buildings well after midnight. But when we walked down the sidewalk like this, arms draped over our shoulders like scarves, eyes met us with a gaze I wasn't accustomed to. When I walk down the sidewalk alone, I pass for a straight woman. This is dicey enough: as a straight woman, I rarely feel entirely safe. Company helps, safety in numbers. A female friend can do the job, sort of; a male friend can make me forget myself. But in the company of Ash, I felt as though a sinkhole waited under the asphalt. *Does Ash feel this all the time? Is this what it's like in the gender of their skin?* The minute the wrong person sees that Ash is not a man, they're something even worse than a woman.

$*$

We went to my house, and at the front door I took their hand and led them down the hall. I switched on the lamp, kissed their upper lip first and then their lower. Ash tugged at my shirt where it knotted in the back. Under their T-shirt they wore a sports bra, and I slid a finger under the elastic in front, up where the skin rose gently, like a foothill, to Ash's breast. They unfastened their watch, knelt to step out of their jeans. Ash's breasts were small and neat, like a textbook drawing of breasts, two curves as tidy as the arc of a bow. I'd never felt the length of a woman's body against me like this, nothing in between. I felt chosen, a woman chosen by a choosy creature, another woman. We were equal. I began to wonder then what we even were, women or just humans, and then I realized I didn't care enough to finish the thought. We slept all night with our toes touching.

Early the next morning Ash appeared beside the bed, standing, and bent close to my face: *I loved last night. Thank you.*

I texted them later. *I loved waking up next to you*, I said. *I felt lucky.*

Ash replied with two blushing emoji faces. *Are we officially dating?* they asked. *I think so.*

I hope so, I said. *Please?* My fingers flew over the keypad.

Yes!! they replied.

I had a phone consultation that morning with a divorce lawyer, a man recommended by our corporate attorney. We talked for exactly eleven minutes, and it felt oddly straightforward, maybe too easy. He said it sounded like Brandon and I agreed upon most everything, which made us good candidates for an uncontested divorce. I wondered when it would feel real, the concept of our divorce.

I went to therapy. I wanted to feel giddy still from my night with Ash, but by afternoon I did not. My head jangled, an almost audible rattle.

As soon as I'd put down the phone, I said, I felt critical of Ash. It was almost like my vision changed: I pulled up a photo of Ash on my phone, giddy to study the face of "my girlfriend," and now it had no impact at all. Yesterday it would have made my eyes roll back with pleasure. I hate this feeling, I told him. I remember it from when I was dating Brandon. It scares me.

Of course it does, my therapist said.

It's like I can let myself be open going in, and then it gets harder just at the point when I always thought it would get easier. Like, I can't hold on to the glee of it.

Well, let's look at Nora, he said. You made yourself busy trying to do everything the right way, trying to win her love. That might have given you, in a sense, a feeling of control. That's not the case with Ash. Ash is clear: they are telling you who they are and what they want. Ash met your ex-husband at a dance party, and Ash still wants you. Maybe they even want all of you, what about that? Maybe they even want the parts you don't want them to see.

27

My mother turned seventy in late November, and to celebrate, she and I took June to New York City for three days. Brandon flew separately to his parents' house in New Jersey, and we all met there for Thanksgiving. Upon our arrival I broke out in hives. At least by now I knew which antihistamine to buy. My mother and I slept downstairs in the guest room that Brandon and I used to sleep in, and he took his childhood bedroom upstairs. June was thrilled for a slumber party with her grandparents. His mother commended us on the whole situation, said how glad she was that we'd come. But I don't know how you think you'll do this, she added, once you have other people in your lives.

I made my usual biscuit recipe and he, his garlic mashed potatoes. At his aunt's house, we sat around a long table decorated with flowers and ribbons and turkey-shaped sugar cookies. June darted from the kids' table to my lap and back, and when it was time to say what I was thankful for, I cried into her hair. I remember thinking that night that our marriage hadn't failed. We were succeeding, if on different terms from the ones we'd set out with.

Ash and I had been dating for six weeks. For all my interest in staying casual, that's not what we were. We were falling in love. To love Ash felt easy, inevitable, and I made no move to stop. But I was afraid. *Well*, I thought, *you wanted to know what it was like to love and be*

loved by a woman, didn't you? Here you are. But how was I supposed to trust what I wanted, when I knew very well that what I wanted could change?

I took solace in the fullness of our lives—that between Ash's work schedule and my custody schedule, we rarely saw each other more than once a week. I needed breathing room, a safe distance from which to study Ash, to believe in what I felt. The week of Thanksgiving, Ash was with family in California, and I liked missing them. I wanted them closer.

A couple of weeks before Christmas, I asked if they wanted to meet June. Ash came over one Sunday, late afternoon. We wouldn't make a big thing of it. June was fresh from the bath, and she sat on my bed in her pink fleecy bathrobe, watching a show on the iPad and eating sheets of dried seaweed the size of playing cards. Ash and I stood in the doorway.

This is my friend Ash, I said, and June looked up from the screen. She was sleepy, couldn't be bothered. Ash waved and grinned and said, Whatcha watching? June shook a piece of seaweed in greeting. In the hall Ash squeezed my arm and beamed. I'm so excited, they whispered. Thank you.

The days shortened, gaining speed. It was nearly Christmas. I got a two-week teaching job near Toronto, my longest stretch away from June. Brandon and my mother gamely stepped in to pick up my slack, but I beat the shit out of myself about it. The timing was wrong: June cried for me; the restaurant needed me for payroll and scheduling; I knew I never should have gone.

Ash and I fought the day before I left. I'd told them that, on a grocery run, I'd picked up an extra box of dishwasher detergent for Brandon's apartment, having seen a few days earlier that he was out.

You know, you don't have to take care of him anymore, Ash said.

I'm not *taking care of him*, I snapped. I'm just being considerate. Am I not allowed to be considerate?

That's not what I'm saying, Ash sputtered. I just—just, you've told me what your pattern was with him. How you felt like you were always taking care, like no one else would do it if you didn't.

What I really want is for you to say nothing negative to me about Brandon, I said. Ever. I can't stand it.

When I arrived in Toronto, I saw that Ash had sent a long text: *You are doing so much. You've been flying back and forth across the country over the last month and have managed to remain a steadfast, attentive mother. You've survived a case of hives. You've managed a restaurant from afar. You are curious and caring, committed to relationship and friendship. I want you to know that I admire you. Thank you for sharing yourself with me in all of it. I see you. I'm here.*

"When you look at yourself in the mirror," writes author Ursula K. Le Guin, "I hope you see yourself. Not one of the myths."[39] I was trying.

On a walk in our heavy coats, a friend commented: You seemed to disappear when you were dating Nora, and you haven't with Ash. That seems like a good thing.

I could feel it too. It's weird, I said to my friend. I never fell in love with a man *because* he was a man, you know? I mean, I wasn't falling in love with a penis. I loved his body because it was his. And I don't think I was drawn to Nora because she was a woman, exactly. I don't think I want a woman *because* she is a woman. Ash is not a woman in the same way I am, but they're also not a man. And I like that so much. That they're making their own form of person—like, this person who is themself.

My friend nodded, said: I'm so happy for you.

I couldn't tell if she understood. But I was happy too.

28

"I eliminated gender, to find out what was left." This was how Le Guin explained her creation of an androgynous race of humans, the Gethenians, in her novel *The Left Hand of Darkness*. "Whatever was left would be, presumably, simply human."[40]

I liked that so much. Of course: under gender we find the bare thing, the person themself. Of course.

But what about sexual orientation? I wanted to add. What do we find under that? What is left if we eliminate orientation—or if it changes willy-nilly? Is there anything solid to me at all, anything I can count on? I'd tried to interrogate myself—had parked myself under fluorescent lights in the cinderblock room of my history, went after myself like Vincent D'Onofrio on *Law & Order*. I wanted a voiceover, some deep baritone: *What do we make of our unreliable narrator? She would have swapped anything, even her sanity, to make sense.*

It was January, and I was Swiffering the bedroom when I saw it, the book I'd bought in the fall: *Sexual Fluidity: Understanding Women's Love and Desire*. The capsule description was a firm handshake: "Having tracked one hundred women for more than ten years," it read, "Lisa M. Diamond argues that for some women love and desire are not rigidly heterosexual or homosexual, but fluid, changing as women move through the stages of life, various social groups and, most importantly, different love relationships."[41] I read it in two days, while June was at Brandon's.

The premise was this: in the course of her career, Diamond, a professor of psychology and gender studies at the University of Utah, had read countless studies of sexual orientation. She noticed that the overwhelming majority had recruited only men as their subjects.[42] As a pregnant woman and new mother, I had been baffled by how little we know of women's bodies; apparently, we know little of their sexuality either.

The studies Diamond read had built and upheld a born-this-way model of sexual orientation, the longtime prevailing model. But since the studies had looked only at men, Diamond wondered how well the model fit non-heterosexual women. So over the course of a decade, she conducted her own methodical study. What she found surprised even her: among female subjects, the norm was not stability in sexual attraction and identity but *change*. Most women reported having a certain orientation, as men did, but their attractions were more nuanced, layered, sensitive to circumstance. Diamond called this quality "fluidity."

Her study dialogued with others, too, that were similarly affirming. Diamond cited a 2000 article by psychologist Roy Baumeister suggesting that women's sexuality is more "plastic" than men's, in the sense not only of variability in sexual attraction, but also in sex drive, qualities they like in a partner, and what they like in bed.[43] (I imagine this will shock absolutely zero women.)

"The notion of female sexual fluidity," writes Diamond, "suggests not that women possess no generalized sexual predispositions but that these predispositions will prove less of a constraint on their desires and behaviors than is the case for men."[44]

This made my eyes well, though for most of my life, I probably would have nodded politely at Diamond's assertion and then privately, internally, scoffed. *Riiight. Explain it however you want. Clearly these people were closeted, and now they're just coming out.* That's what I'd thought when I heard about people who lived for years in the straight world—acquaintances, strangers, celebrities like Cynthia Nixon—coming out as gay or lesbian. I'd had a similar feeling upon hearing of seemingly straight women dating a lesbian for a while and then going back to men. *She was just experimenting.* I wouldn't have believed me.

Both women and men who deviate from the born-this-way model have historically been presumed to be exceptions and weirdos. People whose sexual identity and behavior didn't fit neatly into categories—or whose attractions were not consistently same-sex or other-sex—have been routinely excluded by researchers or tossed out of studies of sexual orientation.[45] Bisexuality has been, for this reason among many, consistently understudied—leaving us, writes Diamond, with a distorted and incomplete understanding of the nature and development of sexual orientation.[46]

But the "exceptions" no longer look exceptional to some researchers, like Diamond. Some have come to view female and male sexual orientation as wholly different phenomena. They begin from the acceptance of paradox, rather than try to explain it away. From this starting point, Diamond posits a new foundational principle: that one of the defining features of female sexual orientation is its fluidity, or a "situation-dependent flexibility in sexual responsiveness."[47] This flexibility means that, regardless of their overall sexual orientation, women may find they experience desires for men or women (or, presumably, any gender) as they move through life, encountering different situations and relationships.

Diamond's study isn't without problems: Who is she referring to, I wish I could ask, when she uses the word *women*? Who, by her lights, is "female"? Does her model of sexual fluidity apply to both ciswomen and transwomen? What about those for whom gender means more than "male" or "female"—who are intersex, genderfluid, non-binary? Diamond's book was published in 2009, barely over a decade ago, but surely her study would be structured and executed differently today, when we talk with dazzling precision and nuance about gender and sexuality spectrums, when the *New York Times* celebrates Pride with a glossary of LGBTQ+ terminology, twenty-two words and growing.[48]

Still, Diamond's work meant something to me. I took pictures of passages and texted a blizzard of them to my friend Matthew, who'd been listening to me grapple since jury duty with what I could now giddily call my "fluidity." Diamond's writing is often impassioned, and I liked it. I felt set on fire by it, elated by not only the affirmation of her findings but by their specificity.

Diamond combs through theories on the biological roots of sexual orientation, studies of genetics and of prenatal hormone exposure. Though no one yet agrees on a clear biological basis for sexual orientation, she notes that female homosexuality seems to have different paths of causation from male homosexuality. If this is so, it makes sense, then, that same-sex sexuality would unfold differently for women and men over their lifespans—and not only because of biology, but because women and men encounter wildly differing social and cultural contexts as their sexuality develops.[49] Among those who are not heterosexual, Diamond found few features of development that were *not* differentiated by gender. It's common in studies of sexual orientation for gay men to report feeling "different" in childhood, as well as having early attractions to other men. But in Diamond's study, fewer non-heterosexual women recall similar experiences. Women also show greater variability in the age at which they notice same-sex attractions, question their sexuality, pursue sex with other women, and first identify as non-heterosexual. And not all women are equally fluid. The same way that women might have different baseline orientations, Diamond found them differently sensitive to situations that could lead to attraction,[50] differently impacted by outside factors that could, depending on one's disposition, speed up or slow down the expression of fluidity.[51]

In addition to the passages I'd sent to Matthew, I texted a barrage of Diamond quotes to a gay male friend. I knew he felt he was born gay, but he'd been sympathetic to my experience.

This reinforces an idea that I have, he wrote back, which is that sexuality and gender are highly individualistic in many ways. We try to make everyone who is "queer" fit some idea of what we think that means. But queerness should really make us realize that the common thread is only that we are all unique. And our sexuality is personal and specific, and it can evolve, just as we do in non-sexual ways.

Whatever a person makes of Diamond's binary read on gender, her findings feel necessary. Rigorous data about female sexuality is still rare, and young women need and deserve accurate information.

"Many of the women in this study," Diamond writes, "expressed embarrassment when explaining changes in their sexual feelings, relationships, or identities because they had internalized the prevailing cultural message that such experiences were highly atypical."[52] Many non-heterosexual women end up feeling "doubly deviant, their experiences reflecting neither mainstream societal expectations nor perceived norms of 'typical' gay experience."[53]

But then I am frightened, too, of how conservatives might weaponize the notion of sexual fluidity. Part of me wants to keep it quiet, a nod between initiates. A good portion of my ease in coming out has rested on the fact that most Americans now accept the born-this-way narrative, that being queer is as much a part of one's basic makeup as being straight is. If we weren't born this way, what ground could we stand on? How many will see an opportunity to conflate "change" and "choice"?

As kids we used to talk about what we'd be when we grew up, as though we would reach a destination of being, a pinnacle to our striving. Nothing about adulthood—not the death of people I cared about, not a lurching entry into business ownership, not even motherhood—had diminished that conviction for me. I believed it completely, wholeheartedly, until I saw Nora. Even if, I wanted to know, *if* I accepted the idea that sexuality can be pliant—at least for some of us, some women, me—why couldn't I go back to how I was before?

Sure, says Diamond, but humans undergo plenty of powerful psychological changes that they do not choose and cannot control. Change, choice, and control are not the same. Think of puberty, she writes. *Think of everything*, I penciled in the margin.

Not a single woman in Diamond's sample, not even those who reidentified as straight or wound up with male partners, voiced regret about her same-sex experiences. "To the contrary, the vast majority were grateful for having had the opportunity to reflect deeply on their emotional and physical desires and to explore their own capacity for intimacy. Whether society chooses to support or punish such opportunities, of course, is up to us."[54]

29

On January 11, 2017, five months after Brandon moved out, we had our first and only meeting at the divorce attorney's office. I wore my favorite pants. We carpooled. In a windowless conference room downtown, with silk flowers and cherry-wood furniture polished to a high gloss, our attorney walked us through the details of an uncontested divorce in the state of Washington. It took ninety minutes. I remember the attorney's surprise when we agreed to assume our own credit card debts, and when Brandon absolved me of responsibility to help pay down his undergrad student debt. This was debt he'd incurred before we met, and it seemed logical that it should stay his.

This is not my business, said the attorney, but you two get along so well. Are you sure you want to get divorced?

We were stupidly proud of his strange compliment.

Still, I was aware of the trust we had for each other, that somehow it was intact. The particulars of our split—that a discrete event had precipitated it, and that we had moved quickly toward divorce—had spared us some of the hurts that accumulate when a relationship breaks down and isn't laid decisively to rest. It is grueling to work through difficult feelings, but I couldn't stomach the exhaustion of letting them linger. We'd had the huge privilege of therapy, among a whole teetering pile of other privileges. Neither of us was interested in vengeance. We were bound together by June—for better or for worse, for real this time. I hoped the fact of her would motivate us to work hard on whatever we had left.

I cried only when we talked through the parenting plan. Dividing up hours and holidays with our child seemed as vicious, as unthinkable, as severing a limb. With our custody arrangement, I would miss half of our daughter's childhood. I attempted to cheer myself with a sobering fact: *So do many (most?) parents who work full-time.* I should feel lucky for my freedom, contingent as it is on my child's father being a willing, reliable, and enthusiastic co-parent. I would rarely worry about June when she was not with me. I want her to love her father. She should.

The attorney finished our paperwork and filed it the next day. This would start the clock on a ninety-day mandated waiting period, and then we could formally divorce.

I mourned the idea of us. Like Orion's Belt, like all the shapes we see fixed against the sky at night, our marriage was a perception dependent upon belief. I had stopped believing, but something solid remained. Brandon only lived on the other side of town. I had a key to his apartment, and he had a key to my house. We took June out together sometimes for soup dumplings and dry-fried green beans. He sent text transcripts of funny things she said. I sent photos of her crossing her eyes.

You know, my therapist said, you can leave a relationship healthy. You don't have to destroy it. I remember he paused, then added: And you don't have to destroy yourself.

The

Three

Squeezes

30

I wrote a list in the notes function of my phone and titled it "2 things to not compromise on."

> *Item 1: Do not marry someone who will not go to therapy, both on their own and with you. Refusing to go to therapy with your partner is like looking the other way when they're drowning.*

> *Item 2: Do not marry someone who does not take active steps to have an egalitarian domestic relationship. Daily tidying of the house, keeping track of grocery needs, buying dog food, etc.*

Maybe interesting, more than anything, that I even thought of marriage.

Another list from that time: *big happiness, big unknowns, big fatigue, big everything.*

I ran into Nora one February morning. We hadn't seen each other since the previous September, the day we broke up. I was standing on a street corner, waiting to cross, when I heard someone call my name. We exchanged the usual pleasantries. I had something I wanted to say and wasn't sure if I should say it. My chest was tight.

You know, I said, I don't believe anymore a lot of the things you told me. It really confused me, that stuff you said about what queer sex is and isn't. It really messed me up.

I know, she said. I'm really sorry.

I'm good in bed, I said. I figured that out: I'm actually very good. A man passed on the sidewalk behind us.

Can I give you a hug? she asked. I said sure. The back of her sweater was cool and rough under my hands, like the face of a cliff. Across the street, the walk sign flashed. Gently I pulled away, waved, and went on.

In King County, Washington, if you are divorcing with children, you must attend a fluorescent-lit seminar called "What About the Children?" It provides information that every parent divorcing should think about: what hurts and helps children during family transitions, how parental conflict affects a family, how to best communicate with co-parents, and the nuts and bolts of drafting a parenting plan. But the pointed title of the seminar made me livid. I felt scolded by it, as though I could possibly *forget* to think about my child.

In the essay "The Bathroom," Zadie Smith writes of her mixed feelings about her father's deferring of his own ambitions for the sake of his family. "*For the sake of the children* was a phrase I especially detested; it seemed a thing people said to get out of the responsibility of actually living out their own desires and ideas."[55]

The data I encounter most often—in the seminar and in the media—insists out that kids of divorce will have it harder than kids whose parents stay married. This truism is obviously true for many. But a lot of us believe nowadays that divorce is no worse for kids than a prolonged unhappy marriage. Is that true? And is it denial or healthy skepticism that makes me want to ask?

Much of the early research around divorce was published in the 1960s and '70s. Much of it measured the well-being of a group of people who were dealing with tremendous social stigma—and whose marriages must have been so bad that the stigma of divorce was preferable to staying. Back then, courts often awarded sole custody to mothers, who were both single and earned little, so children were left with few resources.[56] My divorce, too, would present some financial hardship. I have had to lean regularly on savings; to budget closely, slashing items that once mattered to me; and to accept less stability than I previously had. But my divorce has not left me impoverished.

More recent studies comparing sole-custody and joint-custody arrangements pull up more nuanced findings: that having close relationships with both parents is "the best predictor of future outcomes for the kids [of divorce]."[57] In other words, if you've got to get divorced, yes, there will be pain and loss for everyone involved. But that's not the final word, so long as we let the pain motivate us to love our children—and to let their other parent love them too.[58]

"It's in the nature of the beast that no one gets out of a family unit whole or with everything they want," writes Zadie Smith. "[T]he truth is 'the family' is always an event of some violence. It's only years later, in that retrospective swirl, that you work out who was hurt, in what way, and how badly."[59]

Of course, this looks good on paper, but it doesn't stick, keeps sliding off.

I brought June into this. I brought her into a marriage that had cracks early on, but we ignored them and had her anyway. She is now a child of divorce.

But what's the alternative? That she didn't exist at all?

My therapist gives me homework. Look in the mirror, he says. Really look at yourself. Make eye contact. And say, "I forgive you." Do it every day until our next session.

It's like a prescription: take one tablet by mouth daily for fourteen days. Except that when a doctor writes me a prescription, I follow it exactly. This, I only manage to do twice, furtively, when no one else is around to hear.

The morning of May 25, 2017, was a "parent tea" in June's class at school. Brandon and I both went, and the three of us sat together at a low table in the classroom. There was a bud vase in the center of the table with a single too-tall stem flopping jauntily from its mouth. June had arranged it for us, and now she would serve us cups of lukewarm peppermint tea that sloshed a little as she walked. We'd received an email the week before, saying that her teacher was leaving at the end of the year to get a degree in child psychology. When she stood to thank us, a sob rose in my throat like a cough and I mashed my lips together so hard, they kept aching even after I stopped.

After the tea, Brandon and I drove separately to King County Superior Court. The attorney was waiting for us upstairs, at the end of a grim marble-lined hallway, and he led us into a room with pews, an unlikely chapel, that faced a long counter at the front. We sat down in a pew at the back, and the attorney offered us sticks of gum. When an attendant called our names, we filed up to the counter where the judge flipped through our file. He asked us to confirm our names, and we did, and then he asked, Is your marriage irretrievably broken? In unison we said yes. Then the judge signed something, or stamped something, I don't remember, and handed the papers to our attorney. Out in the corridor, the attorney slid the file into a slot in the wall. It was done. We all shook hands, and that was it. But it seemed wrong to go back to the world; we were tender as newly molted crabs. So we walked through downtown, along streets we'd crossed on our first date twelve years earlier, and wound up at a friend's restaurant, where they bought us a noontime glass of Champagne.

31

A week and a day later, Ash had top surgery. They'd thought on it for more than a year, and less actively for decades; breasts had never seemed to belong on their body. Ash wore a sports bra for the compression, the way it flattened their silhouette. In the short time we'd been together, I had noticed their discomfort with wearing even that—not because it dug or pinched but because it pointed to the fact that they had breasts at all.

I was nervous when Ash told me they wanted finally to do something about it. What do you think? they asked. I love your breasts, I said. To be honest, I want more time with them. But I also want you to have *your* body.

I went with them to a consultation at the plastic surgeon's office. We didn't mention that we'd been together for only seven months. I sat in the waiting room while Ash was in surgery, then brought them to my house to recover. When June joined us the following day, she and I promptly came down with fevers, and the three of us spent the weekend at various degrees of supine, lined up against the headboard of the bed like a display of broken-down dolls. I was exhausted; it was too much. I was angry at myself for taking this on a week after our divorce. I should have let Ash recuperate at their own apartment. But then there would be moments. June was fascinated by the surgical drains, the grenade-shaped bulbs that hung from skinny plastic tubes draped over Ash's shoulders. She wanted to watch Ash empty them, an event that sent me hiding in the living room.

Why did you have your boobs taken off, again? I heard June's voice from the bathroom. We'd talked casually with her, a few times, about how some people are boys, and some people are girls, and some people don't really feel like either, and some people feel like both.

Well, replied Ash, having boobs just didn't seem like *me*. Have you ever put on a shirt, or maybe pants, that didn't feel like "you"? And that you wanted to take off, because you didn't like how you felt in them?

I sat on the sofa and grinned, listened to them chitchat like old friends.

One morning I left early to teach a workshop. June was kneeling on the floor in front of the kitchen cabinets, pulling out a ziplock baggie to fill with coins she'd been collecting. She and Ash were going on an adventure: the pancake house, then the zoo. June was excited to buy something from the gift shop with her money. Later in the afternoon, we'd work in the yard, and I'd water Fairy Meadow, June's name for the still-bare patch of dirt where the sewer guys had dug to access the line. We'd scattered some wildflower seeds there, though I realized as we did it that I hadn't prepared the soil. We were dumping seeds on dry, baked dirt. But June was very protective of Fairy Meadow and didn't want anyone to step on it, not even the dog. Sometimes when she was asleep I wanted to go outside in secret, work the soil properly, and replant it, make it all work out for her.

I thought often about what I wanted June to learn or take away, if anything, from those months. I remember thinking once that the most important thing I wanted was for her to understand what it meant to empathize, to be truly kind. Then I changed my mind; that wasn't quite it.

As a child and a young adult, I had watched my mother grieve many deaths. I'd felt panicked when she cried, when she had "sad attacks." But I got to see real human feeling in grown-ups, got to practice that kind of discomfort, got to see that we would survive. When my turn came to be a grown-up with feelings, I had not forgotten. I don't think I ever fell apart in front of June, not apart-apart, but I was grouchy, weepy, tired. When I had the energy, we talked about it, and I tried to explain what she was seeing in me, to put words to my emotions and actions. I wanted to metabolize the grief for both of us, to offer her what she needed—no more and no less—to comprehend what she might feel. I hope she'd understand, as I was coming to understand it, that things might feel groundless, but she was safe.

The weekend of the Fourth of July we went on a camping trip to Lake Wenatchee—me, Ash, and June, with a couple of the Thursday-night dinner families. We didn't have our own tent or sleeping bags, so we borrowed them, and when we arrived at the site, I saw that we were out of our league. The other families had fancy tents and cots, bins full of dedicated cooking equipment for camping, and comfortable, well-designed chairs that folded into stuff sacks. I knew they'd been camping multiple times a summer for years, but it didn't help; they also had *intact marriages*, which was even worse. I woke up in the night, pinned between June and the nylon wall of the tent, and started to cry. I tried not to make any noise, but Ash reached over and touched my shoulder.

You okay? they asked.

I hate all of this, I squeaked. All their perfect lives.

Shhhhhhhhhh, they whispered, rubbing my arm. We'll get through this. We will.

I wrote this down in a notebook. *Happiness : joy :: sadness : suffering. The difference is in intensity and duration.*

I went around and around: Could I have done this all, all these months, differently? But really, *could I?* The merry-go-round was more palatable than what I'd started to suspect: that I would suffer, and that I'd probably make other people suffer too, because I couldn't avoid it. The best-case scenario, then, might be a safe place to do the suffering, and a witness to keep me company. But Jesus, who would agree to that? Who would possibly accompany me? Because if someone agrees to be my witness, then I will have to be theirs too.

32

Marriage had been complicated. Not being married was complicated too. Brandon and I still worked together at Delancey: he was sort of the heart of the place, and I was the head. This arrangement, in fact, was much like our marriage, with all its upsides and downs, affirmation and infuriation. And without the smoothing, binding action of our vows, we got mean, angry, righteous. That summer we were both so tired.

One month, then two, past our divorce, a thought came to me, started to thicken like ice cream on the paddle. *It's like we're still married.* We were trying to be friends, co-parents, and business partners. I couldn't do all three. I would keep "co-parent," and hopefully "friend." But I wanted to leave the business. I didn't want to co-own the restaurant anymore. I wanted to be a writer again, only a writer.

We talk-yelled about it; then we settled down and began to really talk. We sorted out a plan: I would stay another year at the restaurant. I'd train my replacement, help pave the transition, save some money to see me through. We'd noticed years before, as crucial staff members left and moved on, that after the upheaval of losing them, the restaurant was strangely okay, often even better. I hoped, and I had to believe, that this would still hold true.

The next week we flew separately to Memphis, where our friend Ben was getting married—remarried, this being his second marriage.

Brandon and I were tentative with each other, skittish as deer, but we were trying. The day after the wedding, a bunch of us converged on Ben's house to eat reception leftovers. Ben and his wife were leaving the next morning for a honeymoon, and the interior of the house was to be painted while they were gone. They asked for our help in moving the furniture away from the walls, and we broke into teams. I wound up in the master bedroom with Ben, Brandon, and a couple of others.

I like this bed frame, Brandon said, rapping his knuckles on the headboard.

Right? IKEA, said Ben. Not easy to assemble, let me tell you. Putting this thing together was a real testament to our relationship.

Man, I know how that goes, I chimed in from across the room, where I was holding Ben's desk chair. Ash and I assembled an IKEA bed frame over the winter, and I came away feeling like I was married already!

Well, said Brandon. Technically, you were.

There was a beat, and then the three of us boomed into laughter.

When I got home from Memphis, I found a juror summons for Brandon in the mail. I snapped a picture of it and texted it to him.

Maybe I'll meet someone! he texted back.

Brandon's father, June's grandfather, taught her this endearing thing: walking down the street, in the car, or anywhere, he'd reach for her wrist and squeeze it gently, three times. *I. Love. You.* Now we all do it, Ash included. Three squeezes: *I love you.*

I read a profile in the *New Yorker* of the novelist Elizabeth Strout. After her daughter left for college, Strout moved out of the house she'd shared with her then-husband. "I know that one piece was a desire to really just focus on her writing," her ex would tell the *New Yorker*. "A desire to not have to be responsible for anybody else." He and Strout eventually divorced.

"They like each other so much—that made it confusing," said their adult daughter. "My takeaway is that love itself is not enough."[60]

33

The ghosts are sneaky. Making coffee one morning that fall, not long after Ash moved in, I heard a new but oddly familiar sound: *chick-a-dee-dee-dee-dee-dee*, it went. It was the song of a black-capped chickadee perched on the lichen-coated branches of the plum tree outside. I'd read the syllables of the chickadees' song years earlier in *The Taste of Country Cooking*, by Edna Lewis, a book Brandon and I loved so much that, when we were newly married, I'd read passages to him out loud. But I'd never heard the real song, or not that I noticed, until that morning. I'm haunted, I told Ash.

In the winter, Ash took a work trip to Portland, and I drove down to join them. Walking to the restaurant where we planned to meet, I passed a hotel where Brandon, June, and I had once stayed. Now I was the ghost in the scene, lurking on the sidewalk outside, beneath rooms where my life used to be. June had been four months old when we'd stayed here, and I was newly emerged from postpartum depression. As she slept in her Pack 'n Play, a noise machine humming beside her, Brandon and I had sex for the first time since her birth. I knew it would be good for us, and it was. It only hurt for an instant as we started, and I even came. It was fun. I went to use the bathroom afterward, and in the low blue light from the window, I looked at my reflection. *Remember this feeling*, I told myself. Sex not only felt physically good, but it made me feel close to him. I was proud of us, proud of the act itself. In showing up with Brandon this way, after such a hard time, I'd done something not only beneficial for us but also prudent, advisable, like maxing out my Roth IRA contributions for the calendar year.

A friend sent word from amid the trials of her winter: her new baby hadn't been sleeping, and she'd gotten a horrible cold. Her husband took a day off to be with her, and they snuggled in bed. "Marriage is hard," she wrote, "but marriage is also transcendent."

I touched my hand to the hole where my marriage used to be. I peered down the fissure. We were married for ten years. Does it count for anything? Is the counter zeroed now? Who decides if it is? I want us to be the ones to make the call.

We don't always look at each other when we talk, as though our words were for the room and not the other. We've learned to be kind rather than exacting. Sometimes I think he might hate me. On better days, I'm glad for the plasticity of his heart. Our marriage transcended us, and it lives on in this weird, complicated family we make.

I'm reaching now, but I try it: "Divorce is hard, but divorce is also transcendent." If marriage defines a certain set of limitations, is there something transcendent about its end? Is there something out here I couldn't have imagined, past the breach in the perimeter? Out where we are now, beyond the old checkpoints, in the space at the margin?

I am optimistic. But there is freedom too in a degree of pessimism. Brandon and I will do things differently, like we always have. We will disagree in ways that drive each other batshit—and not funny-batshit, just regular. I used to want him to change; I always expected him to change. He might never, but I might not either. I teeter sometimes on the edge of disliking him, let myself sway there a while. It passes, because now I can get up and leave. I can't fix or control everything, but I can also stop trying to. There's freedom in giving up some hope.

I can commit to being a "good-enough" co-parent. I don't know what Winnicott would say, but I like it. I can commit to trying to weather the hiccups and disappointments. Aiming to be good-enough might actually give us a shot at being decent. I can try to loosen my grip on all of us—not just on Brandon, but on Ash and June. Let each of us slip into our places, be what we are. Not because I'm so generous, but because I want them to do the same for me.

Brandon, Ash, and I have gone to family counseling, to keep working at it. Ash and I work at it too. There are days when I wish I could have a brand-new life with Ash, shiny and unblemished—our own family, uninformed by exes and the gymnastics of co-parenting. I don't like that Ash is haunted by my ghosts. It wasn't what they imagined for themself. But this wasn't what I imagined for myself either.

I am starting to believe that the particular *queer*ness of our family suits us. Brandon and I have gone from being two people in love—one version of "family"—to two divorced people with a child in common. This is family too: people bound together by history, even if they don't always like each other a lot. How bleak, and how great.

The

Old

Hunter

34

In the opening pages of *Several Short Sentences About Writing*, Verlyn Klinkenborg draws up a list of five ways by which we humans know what we know about the world around us. The first is clear enough: we are taught. Then there's a subtler kind of teaching: what others say, if we hear it enough, will come to sound like truth. Emotion also educates us; feelings tell us about our surroundings and ourselves. And we learn by doing, in the gauntlet of experience. But one of his categories always catches me up. It is difficult to intuit, because it runs directly against intuition: "What you don't know," he writes, "and why you don't know it, are information too."[61]

In grad school for anthropology, I got very into Foucault's *The History of Sexuality*. I thought it was so *sexy*, how he shot clean like an arrow through concepts that I, in lessons overt and subtle, had learned as truth. Our understandings of bodies, of sexuality, of sex, writes Foucault, are shaped through the ways we talk (or don't talk) about them. Such concepts are not solid at all, but fluid, like clay slip in a plaster mold.

Like most of us—I venture to guess—who are into Foucault in grad school, I read his theories as an invitation to interrogate the world around me, but not so much *myself*. Principles are sexy when you can use them against someone or something; applied to oneself, the effect is less appetizing. I'm the same pliant substance as everyone else.

But this is a slipperiness I find I want to study now, and study gently: observe it as it moves, start to put language to it. There's relief here, in admitting how little I know about myself. I want to believe that there's value in even the attempt to understand. An answer is, in a sense, the result of repeated attempts to seek it, even when those attempts are mistaken; astronomers and mathematicians call this a theory of errors. Determining the position of a moving object like a star or a comet takes repeated observations over time, and each observation will yield slightly different results. Multiple observations tend to conform to a bell-shaped curve, distributing themselves more or less symmetrically around a mean: the likeliest position of the star in question.[62] To ignore my inconsistencies, my pliancy, my "errors," would be a mistake, because at their center is me.

Poking around online, I find a paper by Daniel Dennett, a philosopher, called "The Self as a Center of Narrative Gravity." That puzzling thing, the self, Dennett posits, is analogous to the center of gravity of an object. A center of gravity is an accepted concept in Newtonian physics, but it is not an atom or other physical item in the world. It has no mass or color or physical properties, except for its location in time and space. It is a purely abstract object, Dennett explains, a "theorist's fiction." So too is the self.

When we read fiction, Dennett says, contradictions don't feel like a big deal.[63] We're used to this in stories; we've gotten good at suspending disbelief. It's *just* a fictional character. We find contradictory properties less tolerable, however, when we are trying to interpret real people and things. But contradictory properties are quite normal, something we can all locate in ourselves. Walt Whitman famously exalted in his multitudes.

In the fiction of the self, the self is both author and character. We are constantly writing the novel of ourselves, inventing more and more of it on demand, in response to what the world asks of us. In this way, parts of us that are not exactly known or defined at one time become better defined as we go on creating. We can't undo anything, but we can clarify and interpret. "The past and present wilt," Whitman wrote in "Song of Myself." "I have fill'd them, emptied them. / And proceed to fill my next fold of the future."

I'd wanted so much to have a story that *behaved*, but instead I have a self.

35

It's easier to say what I am not than what I am. I'm not straight. I'm in-between. In a certain sense, maybe I'm not so different from Ash. I find desire where gender crimps to reveal the person underneath it, because that's where I myself want to be found. I'm in-between other identities too: a mother, but only half-time, and a divorced woman who co-parents with her ex.

It doesn't surprise me anymore that Diamond found, among her sample of non-heterosexual women, that "unlabeled" was the sexual identity most frequently used. These women explained that they were increasingly skeptical of the rigid nature of any sexual categorization. Feeling "unlabelable" isn't new, or unusual.

"Fluidity conveys the capacity of women's sexuality to fill an available space the way a body of water takes the form of its immediate boundaries," writes Diamond. "Sometimes the available space is created by a particular environment, opportunity, or relationship, but sometimes it is created by the process of self-reflection. Either way, when the attractions develop, they may be experienced as an expansion and a blossoming rather than as a discovery of something that was always there but just repressed."[64]

In the checkout line at the grocery store I find myself behind a man and a woman with matching tattoos, *till death do us part*, on their forearms. I watched them ring up their ground beef, Pepsi, and corn on the cob, wondering, *How do they do it—commit so deeply that they put it* in *their*

skin? I want to know how. I want to love differently this go-round—to not throw anybody, not even myself, away.

What I want for my queer family is conventional. I want a partner who is home with me for dinner, who is an equal teammate in domesticity and parenting, who goes to bed at the same time I do. From the outside we may not look it, but we are the ordinary partnership I want. As gay artist and writer Joe Brainard said: "If I'm as normal as I think I am, we're all a bunch of weirdos."

I don't know that it's what the rebels at Stonewall were going for. An early post-Stonewall gay-rights organization called the Gay Liberation Front (GLF) had a more radical, revolutionary agenda, which they envisioned enacting through the common efforts of a variety of oppressed groups. The GLF, writes historian Martin Duberman, was "overtly anti-religious, anti-nuclear family, anti-capitalist, and antiwar," as well as anti-racist and anti-patriarchal.[65] But instead of upending these institutions, the broader LGBTQ+ movement has wound up trying to gain access to them. The movement has fought for marriage and military service because a majority of gay Americans have wanted it to do so.

Public attitudes toward LGBTQ+ people, in the United States at least, appear to have shifted dramatically in the half-century since Stonewall, but the gains are not secure. As of this writing, Ash and I have the right to get married, but a baker in Colorado has the right to refuse to make us a wedding cake. Black transwomen face violence of epidemic proportions. According to the Trevor Project, LGBTQ+ youth contemplate suicide at almost three times the rate of heterosexual youth.[66] Even in Seattle, our progressive West Coast home, my security as a non-straight person rests on my whiteness, my being cisgender, and on the fact that I am not poor.

36

In the last years of her life, Ursula K. Le Guin published an essay in which she contemplated the formation of social institutions and their relationship to the sexes. Male solidarity, she wrote, has been the shaper of government, army, priesthood, and the thing we call the corporation. But as for female solidarity, she notes, "without it human society, I think, would not exist. Female solidarity might better be called fluidity—a stream or river rather than a structure. . . . Instead of rising from the rigorous control of aggression in the pursuit of power, the energy of female solidarity comes from the wish and need for mutual aid and, often, the search for freedom from oppression. Elusiveness is the essence of fluidity."[67]

I wonder about this elusiveness in relation to my non-binary partner, who was assigned female at birth, raised as a girl, and identifies more with women than with men, but is both and neither. Ash's power comes from someplace else.

Androgyny is not gender's absence; it's the negotiation made visible. The word *trans* is convenient shorthand for anyone living as a gender other than the one they were assigned at birth, but a person may not be "transitioning"—may not be, as the artist Harry Dodge puts it, on their way anywhere.[68] This is where Ash lives—as sturdy a shelter as any, though frequently pummeled by the elements.

Ash spends more time grooming than I do, and early on it puzzled me. Ash tweezes, blow-dries, gels. It makes sense, because they're more meticulous than I am. They like to look neater than I do. But I think there's also this: as a cisgender woman, I have more wiggle room than Ash does in how we "put on" our genders. Even with the standards that Western culture imposes on cis women, there is more forgiveness for me. Ash has got to stick the landing.

A trans friend says that the period of his transition—between living as a woman and "passing" as a man—was almost too difficult to withstand. When you don't look the way we expect a man to look *or* the way we expect a woman to look, your gender becomes glaring. It was like I was on display, he said; people always asked me to explain. When he started to pass, to blend in among other men, he got his privacy back. The soft marrow of his gender was once again hidden away, like we keep the parts between our legs.

Every few months, I check in with Ash about their pronouns. Does it still feel right when I say *they/them*? It was awkward at first, to raise this conversation; I was afraid of pushing on a sensitive spot. But Ash says they like it when I ask, that it feels like care. It makes us feel close. Now years out from top surgery, Ash's body looks so *right* on Ash, so beautiful and so handsome; it's hard to think of them having ever looked any other way.

All of us, Ash included, have messed up Ash's pronouns. June is usually the one to correct us. I'm grateful to Ash for their grace, for allowing us to falter and figure it out. When I fuck up Ash's pronouns, or anyone else's, I've learned not to make a big deal of it, to just fix it and move on. We each hold up the mirror for the other.

"Why would you be critical of an actual loving human phenomenon, one who lived in the world, always, on her own terms?" wrote Hilton Als of the late Stormé DeLarverie, a butch performer in 1960s and '70s Harlem. "Back in the day, Stormé was the sexiest man I ever met, and what is sex appeal but another quality you can't name, and shouldn't name, especially if you don't want to be fixed by sexual or racial categories? Stormé was herself, which is to say a male self who knew the deal: life will try to limit you if you give in and let it."[69]

Everybody loves that old saw from Heraclitus, that we never step in the same river twice. I prefer its elaboration, by historian of philosophy Daniel W. Graham: The meaning of the river flowing is not that things are changing so that we cannot encounter them twice, but that some things stay the same only by changing.[70]

The same could be said for stars. They're distributed in space in three dimensions, all at different distances from Earth, all with their own independent motions. Their movement is intrinsic to their being; not a single one holds still. Because of this, the constellations we know today will someday be unrecognizable—it will take tens to hundreds of thousands of years, but still. The rate at which a constellation appears to change depends on its distance from us; the closer the stars, the faster they appear to move. Orion is very far away, which means it will still be discernable long after constellations made by closer stars have distorted beyond recognition.

I watched an animation of this on the website for *Popular Mechanics*: the old hunter starts to nod his head until it tumbles between his shoulders, his bow bending and going wonky. There's something comforting to me about this certainty, the undeniability of this change, however unnerving it is to see him go.

Acknowledgments

Thank you to Jamison Stoltz, for his curiosity, his brilliant eye and ear, and his willingness to walk with me through each phase of this project, from reading source material to joining me in the muck of early drafts. Working with him was the kind of editorial experience that people say doesn't exist anymore.

To my agent, Michael Bourret, for his unwavering belief and support, now thirteen years and counting.

For the gift of time, space, and quiet, Deborah Harkness and the Next Chapter, where much of this book was written. Deb, your generosity is staggering, a gorgeous thing. To Sarah Searle and Ben Sedlins, for the cabin at Quartzwood and a week of your care. To Jim Henkens, for a weekend at Lummi and crab in the fridge. And to Amy Wheeler of Hedgebrook, for connecting me with Deb.

To Jean Hindle, for moving me. To Kate Wallich and Dance Church, for returning me to my body, again and again.

To the Thursday Night Dinner Crew, a steadfast chosen family. To Brian Ferry, for always getting it. To friends who've taken walks with me, sent articles and stories, talked shop with me, and buoyed my spirits. To my students, whose guts and smarts teach me so much. To my therapist, Joe.

To the teachers, babysitters, and family friends whose devotion to and love for June enabled me to write this book. Especially to the entire Burmeister-Steinman family; Heidi Rogers, Shawn Muller, and Julian Muller-Rogers; Deb Olson; Annie Noonan; and Allison Winzenried.

For insight, tough and vital questions, and encouragement on the first full draft: Laurie Amster-Burton, Sam Schick, and Angela Garbes.

This book would not exist—not in anything resembling this form, and probably not at all—without Matthew Amster-Burton. First reader, colleague and companion, midwife of words and chapters, my best friend.

For trusting me and being a wonderful father, Brandon.

For being a remarkable parent, grandmother, and human being, my mother, Toni. I'm lucky beyond language to be your daughter.

To Alice, for turning me into the kind of person who thanks her dog in the acknowledgments.

To Ash, for learning with me; for loving me and loving June; for creating space for this story; for showing me every day what partnership can be.

And to June, for making me a mother, for making me brave.

Notes

1. Wisława Szymborska, *Poems: New and Collected, 1957-1997* (New York: Harcourt, 1998), 111.

2. Calvin Trillin, *About Alice* (New York: Random House, 2006), 6.

3. Anne Truitt, *Daybook: The Journal of an Artist* (New York: Scribner, 1982), 26.

4. Neil Genzlinger, "The Problem with Memoirs," *New York Times*, January 28, 2011, https://www.nytimes .com/2011/01/30/books/review/Genzlinger-t.html.

5. Alain de Botton, "Why You Will Marry the Wrong Person," *New York Times*, May 28, 2016, https://www.nytimes .com/2016/05/29/opinion/sunday/why-you-will-marry-the -wrong-person.html.

6. Paul M. Sutter, "The Power of the Wobble: Finding Exoplanets in the Shifting of Starlight," *Universe Today*, November 20, 2018, https://www.universetoday .com/140581/the-power-of-the-wobble-finding-exoplanets -in-the-shifting-of-starlight.

7. Minnie Bruce Pratt, *S/HE* (Los Angeles: Alyson Books, 2005), 11.

8. Alison Bechdel, *Fun Home* (New York: Mariner Books, 2007), 118.

9. Bill Kenkelen, "Losing Son to AIDS Causes Couple to Reach Out," *National Catholic Reporter* (May 25, 1990).

10. Rebecca Solnit, "A Short History of Silence," *The Mother of All Questions: Further Reports from the Feminist Revolutions* (Chicago: Haymarket Books, 2017), 29.

11. This was the statistic often cited at the time, though of course no poll will ever determine precisely what percentage of the human population is non-straight; countless factors encourage underreporting.

12. It is worth noting that, at least through the early 2000s, studies of sexual orientation rarely mentioned bisexuality or other identities falling outside the categories of "gay" and "straight," and individuals

whose experiences didn't fit into these binary categories were regularly excluded from such studies. Such identities were considered anomalies: cop-outs, confusions, or way stations between gay and straight. For further discussion of this, see Lisa Diamond's *Sexual Fluidity*, as well as Movement Advancement Project (MAP)'s 2016 report "Invisible Majority: The Disparities Facing Bisexual People and How to Remedy Them."

13. I overlooked this in high school, because it confused me, but the methodology and conclusions of such studies were widely questioned. In fact, there is much evidence to contradict these findings. Most researchers today reject theories that posit a simple origin of homosexuality, such as a "gay gene." It's likely that we'll never know, on a scientifically verifiable level, what, if anything, determines sexual orientation.

14. A. K. Summers, *Pregnant Butch: Nine Long Months Spent in Drag* (Berkeley, CA: Soft Skull Press, 2014), 12.

15. It is now California College of the Arts.

16. Annie Dillard, *The Writing Life* (New York: HarperCollins, 1989), 32.

17. Esther Perel, "As Marriage Standards Change, A Therapist Recommends 'Rethinking Infidelity,' " interview by Terry Gross, *Fresh Air*, NPR, December 13, 2017, https://www.npr.org/templates/transcript/transcript.php?storyId=570131890.

18. André Aciman, *Call Me by Your Name* (New York: Farrar, Straus and Giroux, 2007), 43.

19. Maggie Nelson, *The Red Parts: Autobiography of a Trial* (Minneapolis, MN: Graywolf Press, 2016), 155.

20. Judith Butler, "Performative Acts and Gender Constitution: An Essay in Phenomenology and Feminist Theory," *Theatre Journal* 40, no. 4 (December 1988): 519-31, http://seas3.elte.hu/coursematerial/TimarAndrea/17a.Butler,performative%5B1%5D.pdf.

21. D. W. Winnicott, "Transitional Objects and Transitional Phenomena—A Study of the First Not-Me Possession," *The International Journal of Psychoanalysis* 34 (1953): 89-97.

22. Truitt, *Daybook*, 74.

23. Mary Oliver and Molly Malone Cook, *Our World* (Boston: Beacon Press, 2009), 73.

24. Pratt, *S/HE*, 35.

25. Rachel Cusk, *A Life's Work* (New York: Picador, 2001), 7.

26. Angela Garbes, *Like a Mother: A Feminist Journey through the Science and Culture of Pregnancy* (New York: Harper Wave, 2018), 10.

27. Sarah Manguso, *300 Arguments* (Minneapolis, MN: Graywolf Press, 2017), 82-83.

28. Ibid., 36.

29. Eve Kosofsky Sedgwick, *Epistemology of the Closet* (Berkeley: University of California Press, 2008), 22-25.

30. Kathy Acker and McKenzie Wark, *I'm Very into You* (South Pasadena, CA: Semiotext(e), 2015), 86.

31. Thomas Leopold, "Gender Differences in the Consequences of Divorce: A Study of Multiple Outcomes," *Demography* 55, no. 3 (June 2018): 769-97, https://www.ncbi.nlm.nih.gov/pmc/articles/PMC5992251.

32. Manguso, *300 Arguments*, 21.

33. Andrea Long Chu, "On Liking Women," *n+1*, issue 30 (Winter 2018), https://nplusonemag.com/issue-30/essays/on-liking-women.

34. "Catalyst," Def. 1, Lexico.com, July 29, 2019, https://www.lexico.com/en/definition/catalyst.

35. Krista Tippett, "Richard Rohr: Growing Up Men," *On Being*, April 13, 2017, https://onbeing.org/programs/richard-rohr-growing-up-men/#transcript.

36. Nelson, *The Argonauts*, 70.

37. Cusk, *Aftermath*, 82.

38. C. G. Jung, "Paracelsus," trans. Gerhard Adler and R. F. C. Hull, in *The Collected Works of C. G. Jung* vol. 15, para. 4, series eds. H. Read et al. (Princeton: Princeton University Press, 1966, original work published 1934).

39. Ursula K. Le Guin, "Bryn Mawr Commencement Address," *Dancing at the Edge of the World* (New York: Grove Press, 1997), 147-60.

40. Ursula K. Le Guin, "Is Gender Necessary? Redux," *Dancing at the Edge of the World* (New York: Grove Press, 1997), 7-16.

41. Publisher description. Lisa M. Diamond, *Sexual Fluidity: Understanding Women's Love and Desire* (Cambridge, MA: Harvard University Press, 2009), retrieved from http://www.hup.harvard.edu/catalog.php?isbn=9780674032262.

42. Diamond, *Sexual Fluidity*, 2.

43. Ibid., 8.

44. Ibid., 24.

45. Ibid., 25-28.

46. Ibid., 28.

47. Ibid., 3.

48. Michael Gold, "The ABCs of L.G.B.T.Q.I.A.+," *New York Times*, June 7, 2019, https://www.nytimes.com/2018/06/21/style/lgbtq-gender-language.html.

49. Diamond, *Sexual Fluidity*, 46.

50. Ibid., 84.

51. Ibid., 88.

52. Ibid., 89-90.

53. Ibid., 15.

54. Ibid., 170.

55. Zadie Smith, "The Bathroom," *Feel Free: Essays* (New York: Penguin Press, 2018), 361.

56. Mandy Len Catron, "Mixed Feelings: Your Divorce Won't Ruin Your Kids," *Rumpus*, May 29, 2018, https://therumpus.net/2018/05/mixed-feelings-your-divorce-wont-ruin-your-kids.

57. Linda Nielsen, "10 Surprising Findings on Shared Parenting After Divorce or Separation," *Institute for Family Studies*, June 20, 2017, https://ifstudies.org/blog/10-surprising-findings-on-shared-parenting-after-divorce-or-separation.

58. Catron, "Mixed Feelings."

59. Smith, *Feel Free*, 362-64.

60. Ariel Levy, "Elizabeth Strout's Long Homecoming," *New Yorker*, May 1, 2017, https://www.newyorker.com/magazine/2017/05/01/elizabeth-strouts-long-homecoming.

61. Verlyn Klinkenborg, *Several Short Sentences About Writing* (New York: Alfred A. Knopf, 2012), 7.

62. Louis Menand, *The Metaphysical Club* (New York: Farrar, Straus and Giroux, 2001), 177-82.

63. Daniel C. Dennett, "The Self as a Center of Narrative Gravity," in *Self and Consciousness: Multiple Perspectives*, eds. F. Kessel, P. Cole, and D. Johnson (Hillsdale, NJ: Erlbaum, 1992), https://ase.tufts.edu/cogstud/dennett/papers/selfctr.pdf.

64. Diamond, *Sexual Fluidity*, 165.

65. Masha Gessen, "Martin Duberman on What the Gay-Rights Movement Has Lost," *New Yorker*, July 9, 2018, https://www.newyorker.com/news/our-columnists/martin-duberman-on-what-the-gay-rights-movement-has-lost.

66. The Trevor Project, "Facts about suicide," https://www.thetrevorproject.org/resources/preventing-suicide/facts-about-suicide/.

67. Ursula K. Le Guin, "A Band of Brothers, a Stream of Sisters," *No Time to Spare: Thinking about What Matters* (New York: Houghton Mifflin Harcourt, 2017), 102-3.

68. Nelson, *The Argonauts*.

69. Hilton Als, "A Pioneer of Gender Performance," *New Yorker*, February 6, 2017, https://www.newyorker.com/magazine/2017/02/06/a-film-on-a-pioneer-of-gender-performance.

70. Daniel W. Graham, "Heraclitus," *The Stanford Encyclopedia of Philosophy* (Fall 2019 Edition), ed. Edward N. Zalta, https://plato.stanford.edu/archives/fall2019/entries/heraclitus/.

Bibliography

Aciman, André. *Call Me by Your Name*. New York: Farrar, Straus and Giroux, 2007.

Acker, Kathy, and McKenzie Wark. *I'm Very into You*. South Pasadena, CA: Semiotext(e), 2015.

Als, Hilton. "A Pioneer of Gender Performance." *New Yorker*, February 6, 2017, https://www.newyorker.com/magazine/2017/02/06/a-film-on-a-pioneer-of-gender-performance.

Bechdel, Alison. *Fun Home*. New York: Mariner Books, 2007.

Belluck, Pam. "Depression During and After Pregnancy Can Be Prevented, National Panel Says. Here's How." *New York Times*. February 12, 2019, https://www.nytimes.com/2019/02/12/health/perinatal-depression-maternal-counseling.html.

Boylan, Jennifer Finney. "What 'Peanuts' Taught Me About Queer Identity." *New Yorker*, February 21, 2019, https://www.newyorker.com/culture/personal-history/what-peanuts-taught-me-about-queer-identity.

Butler, Judith. "Performative Acts and Gender Constitution: An Essay in Phenomenology and Feminist Theory." *Theatre Journal* 40, no. 4 (December 1988): 519-31.

Calhoun, Ada. *Wedding Toasts I'll Never Give*. New York: Norton, 2017.

Call Me by Your Name. Dir. Luca Guadagnino. Perf. Timothée Chalamet, Armie Hammer, and Michael Stuhlbarg. Sony Pictures Classics, 2017.

Catron, Mandy Len. "Mixed Feelings: Your Divorce Won't Ruin Your Kids." *Rumpus*, May 29, 2018, https://therumpus.net/2018/05/mixed-feelings-your-divorce-wont-ruin-your-kids.

Chabon, Michael. *The Mysteries of Pittsburgh*. New York: William Morrow, 1988.

———. *Pops*. New York: Harper, 2018.

Chu, Andrea Long. "On Liking Women." *n+1*, issue 30 (Winter 2018), https://nplusonemag.com/issue-30/essays/on-liking-women.

Cusk, Rachel. *Aftermath: On Marriage and Separation.* New York: Picador, 2012.

———. *A Life's Work.* New York: Picador, 2001.

D'Aulaire, Ingri, and Edgar Parin d'Aulaire. *Book of Greek Myths.* New York: Doubleday, 1962.

de Botton, Alain. "Why You Will Marry the Wrong Person." *New York Times*, May 28, 2016, https://www.nytimes .com/2016/05/29/opinion/sunday/why-you-will-marry-the -wrong-person.html.

Dennett, Daniel C. "The Self as a Center of Narrative Gravity." In F. Kessel, P. Cole, and D. Johnson, eds. *Self and Consciousness: Multiple Perspectives.* Hillsdale, NJ: Erlbaum, 1992, https://ase.tufts.edu/ cogstud/dennett/papers/selfctr.pdf.

Dey, Claudia. "Mothers as Makers of Death." *Paris Review*, August 14, 2018, https://www.theparisreview.org/blog/ 2018/08/14/mothers-as-makers-of-death.

Diamond, Lisa M. *Sexual Fluidity: Understanding Women's Love and Desire.* Cambridge, MA: Harvard University Press, 2008.

Dickinson, Terence. *NightWatch: A Practical Guide to Viewing the Universe.* Ontario, CA: Firefly Books, 2006.

Dieterich, Leah. *Vanishing Twins: A Marriage.* New York: Soft Skull Press, 2018.

Dillard, Annie. *The Writing Life.* New York: HarperCollins, 1989.

Dykema, Jane. "What I Don't Tell My Students about 'The Husband Stitch.'" *Electric Literature*, October 10, 2017, https://electricliterature.com/what-i-dont-tell-my -students-about-the-husband-stitch.

Foucault, Michel. *The History of Sexuality, Vol 1.* Robert Hurley, trans. New York: Random House, 1978.

Galchen, Rivka. "Mo Willems's Funny Failures." *New Yorker*, February 6, 2017, https://www.newyorker.com/magazine/ 2017/02/06/mo-willems-funny-failures.

Garbes, Angela. *Like a Mother: A Feminist Journey through the Science and Culture of Pregnancy.* New York: Harper Wave, 2018.

Genzlinger, Neil. "The Problem with Memoirs." *New York Times*, January 28, 2011, https://www.nytimes.com/2011/01/30/books/review/Genzlinger-t.html.

Gessen, Masha. "Martin Duberman on What the Gay-Rights Movement Has Lost." *New Yorker*, July 9, 2018, https://www.newyorker.com/news/our-columnists/martin-duberman-on-what-the-gay-rights-movement-has-lost.

Giard, Robert. *Particular Voices: Portraits of Gay and Lesbian Writers*. Cambridge, MA: The MIT Press, 1998.

Greenwell, Garth. "The Frog King." *New Yorker*, November 26, 2018, https://www.newyorker.com/magazine/2018/11/26/the-frog-king.

Gross, Terry. "As Marriage Standards Change, A Therapist Recommends 'Rethinking Infidelity.'" *Fresh Air*, December 13, 2017, https://www.npr.org/templates/transcript/transcript.php?storyId=570131890.

Hall, Donald. "Letter in Autumn." *Without*. New York: Houghton Mifflin, 1998, 59-62.

Hanauer, Cathi, ed. *The Bitch Is Back: Older, Wiser, and (Getting) Happier*. New York: William Morrow Paperbacks, 2017.

Hartley, Gemma. *Fed Up: Emotional Labor, Women, and the Way Forward*. New York: HarperOne, 2018.

Hay, Carol. "Who Counts as a Woman?" *New York Times*, April 1, 2019, https://www.nytimes.com/2019/04/01/opinion/trans-women-feminism.html.

Hunt, Samantha. "This Week in Fiction: Samantha Hunt on the Unspoken Terrors of Being a New Mother." Interview by Cressida Leyshon. *New Yorker*, May 15, 2017, https://www.newyorker.com/books/page-turner/fiction-this-week-samantha-hunt-2017-05-23.

Ibsen, Henrik. *A Doll's House and Other Plays*. Peter Watts, trans. New York: Penguin Books, 1965.

Kenkelen, Bill. "Losing Son to AIDS Causes Couple to Reach Out." *National Catholic Reporter*, May 25, 1990.

Klinkenborg, Verlyn. *Several Short Sentences About Writing*. New York: Alfred A. Knopf, 2012.

Le Guin, Ursula K. *Dancing at the Edge of the World*. New York: Grove Press, 1997.

——. *The Left Hand of Darkness*. New York: Ace Books, 1987.

——. *No Time to Spare: Thinking about What Matters*. New York: Houghton Mifflin Harcourt, 2017.

Leopold, Thomas. "Gender Differences in the Consequences of Divorce: A Study of Multiple Outcomes." *Demography* 55, no. 3 (June 2018): 769-97, https://www.ncbi.nlm.nih.gov/pmc/articles/PMC5992251.

Levy, Ariel. "Elizabeth Strout's Long Homecoming." *New Yorker*, May 1, 2017, https://www.newyorker.com/magazine/2017/05/01/elizabeth-strouts-long-homecoming.

Loofbourow, Lili. "The Female Price of Male Pleasure." *Week*, January 25, 2018, https://theweek.com/articles/749978/female-price-male-pleasure.

Lorde, Audre. *Sister Outsider*. Berkeley, CA: Crossing Press, 1984.

Machado, Carmen Maria. "The Husband Stitch." *Her Body and Other Parties*. Minneapolis, MN: Graywolf Press, 2017.

Mackintosh, Sophie. *The Water Cure*. New York: Doubleday, 2019.

Manguso, Sarah. *300 Arguments*. Minneapolis, MN: Graywolf Press, 2017.

Mantel, Hilary. *Giving Up the Ghost*. New York: Picador, 2004.

McColl, Sarah. *Joy Enough*. New York: Liveright, 2019.

McCombs, Theodore. "A Perfectly Normal Interview with Carmen Maria Machado Where Everything Is Fine." *Electric Literature*, April 18, 2019, https://electricliterature.com/carmen-maria-machado-carmilla-lefanu-vampire-interview.

Menand, Louis. *The Metaphysical Club: A Story of Ideas in America*. New York: Farrar, Straus and Giroux, 2001.

Movement Advancement Project (MAP). "Invisible Majority: The Disparities Facing Bisexual People and How to Remedy Them." September 2016, http://www.lgbtmap.org/file/invisible-majority.pdf.

Nagata, Kabi. *My Lesbian Experience with Loneliness*. Los Angeles: Seven Seas, 2017.

Nanette. Written and performed by Hannah Gadsby, 2018. Netflix. https://www.netflix.com/title/80233611.

Nelson, Maggie. *The Argonauts*. Minneapolis, MN: Graywolf Press, 2016.

———. *The Red Parts: Autobiography of a Trial*. Minneapolis, MN: Graywolf Press, 2016.

Nestle, Joan, ed. *The Persistent Desire: A Femme-Butch Reader*. Boston: Alyson Publications, 1992.

Nielsen, Linda. "10 Surprising Findings on Shared Parenting After Divorce or Separation." *Institute for Family Studies*, June 20 2017, https://ifstudies.org/blog/10 -surprising-findings-on-shared-parenting-after-divorce -or-separation.

O'Farrell, Maggie. *I Am, I Am, I Am*. New York: Knopf, 2017.

Oliver, Mary, and Molly Malone Cook. *Our World*. Boston: Beacon Press, 2009.

Orr, Gregory. *Orpheus and Eurydice: A Lyric Sequence*. Port Townsend, WA: Copper Canyon Press, 2001.

Padgett, Ron, ed. *The Collected Writings of Joe Brainard*. New York: Library of America, 2012.

Pratt, Minnie Bruce. *S/HE*. Los Angeles: Alyson Books, 2005.

Rich, Adrienne. *Diving into the Wreck: Poems 1971-1972*. New York: W. W. Norton, 1973.

———. *The Dream of a Common Language, Poems 1974-1977*. New York: W. W. Norton, 1993.

Schulman, Sarah. *Ties That Bind: Familial Homophobia and Its Consequences*. New York: The New Press, 2009.

Sedgwick, Eve Kosofsky. *Epistemology of the Closet*. Berkeley: University of California Press, 2008.

Shapiro, Dani. *Hourglass*. New York: Anchor Books, 2018.

Smith, Zadie. *Feel Free: Essays*. New York: Penguin Press, 2018.

Solnit, Rebecca. *The Mother of All Questions: Further Reports from the Feminist Revolutions*. Chicago: Haymarket Books, 2017.

Solomon, Andrew. *Far from the Tree: Parents, Children, and the Search for Identity*. New York: Scribner, 2012.

Summers, A. K. *Pregnant Butch: Nine Long Months Spent in Drag*. Berkeley, CA: Soft Skull Press, 2014.

Sutter, Paul M. "The Power of the Wobble: Finding Exoplanets in the Shifting of Starlight." *Universe Today*, November 20, 2018, https://www.universetoday.com/140581/the-power-of-the-wobble-finding-exoplanets-in-the-shifting-of-starlight.

Swearingen, Jake. "How the Big Dipper Has Changed—and Will Change—Over 200,000 Years." *Popular Mechanics*, April 11, 2016, https://www.popularmechanics.com/space/deep-space/a20347/how-the-big-dipper-has-changedand-will-changeover-200000-years.

Szymborska, Wisława. "Could Have." *Poems: New and Collected, 1957-1997*. New York: Harcourt, 1998.

Taormino, Tristan. *Opening Up: A Guide to Creating and Sustaining Open Relationships*. Jersey City: Cleis Press, 2008.

Templeton, Joan. "The Doll House Backlash: Criticism, Feminism, and Ibsen." *PMLA* 104, no. 1 (January 1989): 28-40, http://www.jstor.org/stable/462329.

Tippett, Krista. "Richard Rohr: Growing Up Men." *On Being*, April 13, 2017, https://onbeing.org/programs/richard-rohr-growing-up-men/#transcript.

Trillin, Calvin. *About Alice*. New York: Random House, 2006.

Truitt, Anne. *Daybook: The Journal of an Artist*. New York: Scribner, 1982.

Veaux, Franklin, and Eve Rickert. *More Than Two: A Practical Guide to Ethical Polyamory*. Portland, OR: Thorntree Press, 2014.

Whitman, Walt. "Song of Myself." *The Complete Poems*. New York: Penguin Classics, 2005.

Willems, Mo. *Goldilocks and the Three Dinosaurs*. New York: Balzer + Bray, 2012.

Winnicott, D. W. "Transitional Objects and Transitional Phenomena—A Study of the First Not-Me Possession." *International Journal of Psychoanalysis* 34 (1953): 89-97.

Wolf, Naomi. "A Woman's Place." Commencement Address, Scripps College, May 17, 1992, http://gos.sbc.edu/w/wolf.html

Yanofsky, Noson S. "The Ship of Theseus and the Question of Identity." *Utne Reader*, November 2013, https://www.utne.com/mind-and-body/ship-of-theseus-identity-zeOz1311zjhar.

Credits